THOUGHTS ARE THE WAY TO YOUR DESTINY

Bigger Thoughts are the first step to your Success.

The book will help you in realizing that if you are still running in the same rat race and what can you do to be unique and join the very short community of the Richest people in the Whole world.

About The Author

Rishabh Jain is a visionary thinker and passionate advocate for living a life of purpose and fulfillment. He was born on 26th October, 1997 in a Delhi, India. Completed the Education from CBSE Board and started running in the same rat race until he realized. He has spent years studying the intersection of mindset, motivation, and success. Through his own journey of self-discovery and transformation, he has developed a unique perspective on how to overcome obstacles, build resilience, and achieve meaningful goals.

As a writer he has inspired countless individuals to rethink their assumptions about success and happiness. His work has been influenced by thought leaders in the personal development space, and he is dedicated to helping others unlock their full potential and create a life that truly reflects their values, passions, and aspirations.

Rishabh Jain lives in Delhi, India and can be found at rishabhjain1584@gmail.com.

<u>Preface</u>

As we navigate the twists and turns of life, it's easy to get caught up in the chaos of our daily routines and lose sight of what truly matters. But what if we told you that the power to shape your destiny lies within your own mind?

In the following pages, Rishabh Jain shares a profound and practical guide to breaking free from the limitations of the status quo and unlocking the potential that lies within. With a unique blend of insight, inspiration, and actionable advice, this book will challenge you to rethink your assumptions about success, happiness, and the true meaning of fulfillment.

Join Rishabh Jain on a journey of self-discovery and empowerment as you learn to harness the transformative power of your thoughts and turn your dreams into reality. Get ready to unlock your full potential and create the life you've always imagined – a life that truly reflects your deepest desires and highest aspirations."

Table of Contents

Part-1 (10)
Want Success? Change your Mindset

- **Chapter-1 (Reality of Life)**   12
- **Chapter-2 (Difference in thinking of Rich and Poor People)**   17
    1. Rich people do get employees and poor people do get employed.
    2. Assets and Liabilities.
    3. Buy Assets first and Luxuries at Last.
    4. Playing with Taxes.

- **Chapter-3 (Don't work for money, Generate money)**   23
    1. Mind is your biggest Asset.
    2. Learning is an Asset to be Rich.
    3. Story of two young gentlemen.
    4. Rich people work for learning not for money.
- **Chapter-4 (Get Through Challenges)**   31
    1. Managing your expenditure.

- **Chapter-5 (Initial steps to Success)   35**
    1. Results you want.
    2. Make Right Choices.
    3. Limit your surroundings.
    4. Learning should never stop.
    5. Invest in yourself.
    6. Get a Mentor.

Part-2 (44)

Mindset Changed? Let's Start

- **Chapter-1 (Introduction to Business)   46**
    1. Value Creating.
    2. Parts of Business.

- **Chapter-2 (Examining a Business before you start)   51**
    1. Skills should have Economic Values.
    2. Hard rule of Market.
    3. Understanding what people actually want.
    4. Market Evaluation.
    5. Competition.

- **Chapter-3 (Types of Business)   58**
    1. Business based on a product.
    2. Business based on Services.
    3. Asset that need to be created only once.
    4. Services on Rent.

5. Retail Business.
6. Lease.
7. Agency.
8. Gathering people of same Interests.
9. Offering Loan by charging pre-defined Interest Rate.
10. Offering a right to someone in exchange of money.
11. Providing Insurances and Safety Cover.
12. Investing in Other Businesses.

- **Chapter-4 (Major Strategies to run a Business)**   **73**

1. Removing hassle in exchange of charge.
2. Value worth paying for it.
3. Offering Value in different forms.
4. Combining different forms of Value.
5. Being a Mediator or removing the one.
6. Disclose your Idea.
7. Continuous Updates.
8. Getting and Applying Feedback.
9. Expectations before paying for anything.
10. Some more points to consider.
11. Assumptions.
12. Testing before making it available.

- **Chapter-5 (Different Segments of Business)**   **87**

1. Marketing.
2. Sales.
3. Value Delivery.
4. Finance.

Part-3 (124)

<u>Working in the best way.</u>

- **Chapter-1 (How does our Brain work?) 126**
  1. Requirements of working efficiently.
  2. Things under control.
  3. Satisfaction of Life.
  4. Behavioral Change.
  5. Situations where you are unable to get things under control.
  6. Fight between Thoughts.
  7. Learning through Patterns.
  8. Mental Stimulation and Imagination.
  9. Being Motivated and Working for Status.
  10. Fear is stronger than Belief.
  11. Decision Making Power.

- **Chapter-2 (Working as an Individual or with others)   141**
  1. Procrastination.
  2. Multitasking.
  3. Setting right Goals.
  4. Interests and Notice.
  5. Making Commitments.
  6. Working Step by Step.
  7. Fear caused by thoughts.
  8. Overconfidence
  9. Time and Energy
  10. Attractive Ideas and Reality
  11. Loss of Interests.
  12. Comparison and Control.
  13. Continuous Learning.
  14. Influencing or Compulsion.
  15. Limited Team.

16. Showing Respect Equally.
17. Make other people feel good.
18. Task Assignment and Planning.
19. Being in a Group.
20. Role Models.
21. Bound to take action indirectly.
22. Early Judgment.
23. Availability.
24. Solution Oriented.
25. Management and Leadership.
26. Recruitment and Hiring.
27. Equality.

- **Chapter-3 (Understanding and Improving structures of Business)   180**
    1. Flow of Resources.
    2. Analyzing the lack in Stock.
    3. Adaptable to Changes in Environment.
    4. Understanding the connections of Department.
    5. Analyzing different structures and departments.
    6. Neglecting.
    7. Auditing.
    8. Comparison and Analyzing Output.
    9. Changes for Improvement.
    10. Changes in process to get more output and profit.
    11. Analyzing the changes before Execution.
    12. Business on Auto-Pilot.

Part-1

Want Success? Change your Mindset.

This part of the book will help you in changing your mindset and take your initial steps to get on the ladder of your Success and will help you in achieving your Goal and being Rich.

1.

Reality of Life

It is the end of 2015, and a young man has completed his schooling like many other students. This young guy has grown up listening to the very often lectures or learning being given by his middle class parents and society i.e. studying hard and getting good marks in Academics is the only way to success. He is entering the same race of finishing his graduation and obtaining a degree to secure a high-profile job. He has always been average student in his schooling and academics. He always struggled to get good marks in his academics and somehow managed to get through the schooling with Science stream as like many others he has chosen to do B Tech. He has given many entrance exams with the best of his abilities, seeking admission to any recognized universities or colleges.

Regrettably, he was unable to do well in that. At the end, he had to go to another state for further studies where he got admission in a college through management quota (Getting admission by paying some donation amount to the college or university). As previously mentioned, his family is very mediocre. While his father runs a small manufacturing unit, his mother is a homemaker. He has two more members in his family, including his younger sister who is still pursuing her education and his grandmother. It is not easy for his family to afford his further studies. Still, they somehow managed to send him 1554 miles away from his home to complete his further studies. So that he can secure a good job to further support his family.

He joined college and tried his best to get good grades again. Now, the first semester has passed and he is able to see the competition in society. He is able to relate his situation with many other fellow teammates who are running in the same rat race. After the first year, he has managed to achieve good grades. Meanwhile, he came to realize that his family is having a hard time financially supporting him for his studies. After college, he began working part-time and attempted to handle his expenses independently. His studies are greatly impacted by this job. The second year has not yet started, and it is a very crucial time for him and his family. His father suffered a loss in his business, so unfortunately, he had to drop his studies and come back.

> The Trouble with the rate race is that even if you win, you're still a rat.
>
> -Lily Tomlin.

The young man returned and joined his father's small business. Worked with him for a couple of months and supported him. He became frustrated because it wasn't his cup of tea. Soon, he joined a small diploma course with the expectation of getting a full-time job. After the course was completed, he was given a full-time job opportunity. Although the salary is very low in that job, he thought if he worked hard, he would get a promotion at a higher level. Soon, he realized that to get promotions he must be a graduate which again demotivated him a lot. As we all know, the value of a degree is considered to be greater than the value of hard work and knowledge. He changed many organizations due to small salary hikes and became very

> **It is really important to realize that you are running in a rat race to decide your further actions.**

unstable in his career. He never got any promotions and life never gave him a chance to get any recognition in his life. The level of demotivation he is facing is very high in terms of his work life. It is now 2019 and he is working with a recruitment firm. He is trying to save money every month as taught by his father for his future. He is currently competing in a rat race by working 8 hours a day for 6 days a week.

In 2020 and as we all know the world came across a huge Covid Pandemic, which destroyed many families and people not only in terms of life but with finances too. This young man also lost his job and his father's business also went out of business. After spending some of their savings, this young guy managed to get a work from home job again. Now he is being the only guy supporting his family financially. As it happens in many mediocre families, he got married at the age of 24 and became a father at the age of 25. Now he has the responsibility of two more people. On top of that, his father is getting worse day by day, and it is really difficult for him to manage all the things. He has been trapped in the same situation which every middle class person faces in their life. He was literally in a trauma and meanwhile he was thinking that how these rich people get wealth, happiness and peace at the same time. He started exploring and realized that there is one common thing that every rich person does in their routine life. That is reading books regularly and constantly gaining knowledge. This young guy has never like reading books as it seems to be boring to him. However, he still started reading some self-help books and this habit has changed his life drastically.

The name of this Young Guy was Rishabh Jain, The author of this book. I am writing this book to share the learning and some powerful insights using my experiences in my life. This book can help anyone in changing his/her mindset and their life. This book can help anyone to escape from the rat race of mediocre people who are willing to gain an ultimate wealth, happiness and peace in their life.

Notes:

2.

Difference in Thinking of Rich and Poor People.

The first lesson I have learned, has changed my mindset completely. There is a huge difference between the thinking of Rich and Poor people. When I have started exploring, I have realized that the best source of knowledge is always a book. So, I have started reading self-help books. The first book I have read, did blow my mind and did let me see the reality of society. Let me share those eyes opening learning with you.

Rich people do get employees and Poor people do get employed

The so called rat race of working 8-9 hours a day, 5-6 days a week has been generated in the society because of the core element of Fear. This fear let a person to work in a safe zone or a job. The fear of not paying bills, fear of getting loss, fear of starting over, fear of uncertainty and much more. This fear is a hard block or a cataract in one's eye, which doesn't let him see the things the other way around. Most of the society is suffering from this disease named as fear and trying their best to play it safe. Working in a full time Job, getting paid the same amount everyone, managing expenses, trying to save not even thinking that even a job is much riskier than being self-employed which has been proved by COVID Pandemic in 2020.

This is how the mentality of poor and mediocre people works. Now let's take a look at Rich People Thinking.

A Rich person or a normal person with Rich mentality never tries to play it safe. The do not work for a fix salary as they have overcome the fear of getting losses. They do not think of saving money for future. They do not work for 8-9 hours a day for money. They let the money work for them. A poor person or middle class person works for a company to make his company's owner Rich. However, Rich people invest money and hire people to work for them.

Let say if a person is working in a manufacturing unit. He is only able to make 100 units by working 8 hours a day. However, if he hires 100 people to do the same work for 8 hours a day for him and then ultimately he will be able to produce 10000 units a day by working same 8 hours a day. This is the magic of investing and hiring people.

I hope now you guys should be able to see the whole difference between the thinking of Rich and Poor people.

Assets and Liabilities.

Another eye opener lesson for us, Rich people acquire assets and poor people buy liabilities.

To understand this better, we must understand that what it means by assets and liabilities.

In a very simple language, an asset is something which puts money in your pocket (Invest in business, stocks, real estate, bonds, gold etc.). However, a liability is something which takes money out from your pocket (Buying luxuries, personal house, personal car and much more).

A person with poor mentality always buys liabilities, whenever he gets paid for something. He will go ahead and buy a car, a personal house or a holiday trip to a hill station. This is nothing but getting more expenses. These things will only put a person in a shortage of money sometimes in debt too.

> The philosophy of the rich and the poor is this: the rich invest their money and spend what is left. The poor spend their money and invest what is left.
>
> -Robert T. Kiyosaki

However, a Rich person always invest money into Gold, stocks, bonds, real estate or any business. This will get him more money or increase the value of his money. This is how a rich person makes money from money.

I am not saying that buying a car or taking a holiday trip is not good. But these things need to be bought after you make good investments to manage their expenses. The liabilities should be bought from a very small portion of your Income. So, first make enough money and then buy luxuries.

There is one more trap going on, which is buying luxuries on EMI or installments which only puts a person into unnecessary debt. This is only for taking out money from your pocket every month and this way it is really easy for companies to increase their sales. Now, it is up to you how you want to go about.

Buy Asset first and Luxuries at Last.

As I mentioned earlier, Rich people buy assets first and they let all the luxuries to be bought at last. They first improve their asset column and improve their income statement. Once, their income statement shows enough

> "It was considered as being bad enough to be a slave; but to be a poor man's slave was deemed a disgrace indeed!"
>
> -Frederick Douglass

amounts to spend on luxuries than only they buy it. However, a poor person or a middle class person buys liabilities first. They always are in a trap of debt and unnecessary expenditures.

Let's understand this by taking an example. Suppose if you buy a car, as soon as you buy it, it becomes second hand and its value goes down almost by half. Now, if you spend the same money in buying Gold, the value of it will never cut off to half. It might go down slightly according to the market but will always keep you in profit in a long term.

Another point is that poor people work whole life in a job to make someone else Rich. However, the Rich people never work for 8 hours a day in routine life. They hire people to work for them. They invest in a business and smartly put it on autopilot and thinks of doing another investment. A poor person working for his whole life gets nothing at the last.

Meanwhile, if the same person would have a bit courage can do wonders by putting his hard work in a right direction and can get him out of a rat race.

Playing with Taxes.

Tax is something, which is almost can be considered as evil in a middle class society. They always get paid after deduction of all taxes by the companies implied by the Government. Moreover, when they go to buy anything for themselves, there also they would have to pay taxes.

A Rich person always knows how to play with taxes and what are its loop holes. For Rich people, the taxes are being deducted after calculating all the expenses being done by his company. They only get taxed on whatever is left after all the expenses are done. Expenses like cost of production, running a business, business trips, buying things for offices and much more. They get taxed on the amount left after these expenses are done. They do donations more and more to show them as expenses and save taxes.

Employees earn and get taxed before being paid and whatever is left, they get to spend. On the other hand, in an organization they do spending first and then get taxed on whatever is left. That is why companies always keeps on doing further investments as they get tax benefits on them.

Notes:

3.

Don't work for money,
Generate Money.

These are the things which made me think that whatever we were doing in handling our lifestyle was actually wrong. After applying all these lessons in my life, it did magic and made me more confident about our future. Because of these lessons I was able to make some great changes in our way of handling our finances every month. Although it is really hard for me to get those changes instantly as our family has also got all those wrong learning. It will take some time for them to adapt these changes and understand them. Unlearning is always difficult than learning something new. I did cut off the unnecessary expenses which I was bearing every month. Also, I did start making some investments too.

However, the journey doesn't stop here. Investments are not just throwing money anywhere. Otherwise, there will be no difference between Gambling and Investing.

Rich people don't do gambling; they take calculated Risk. They put money in any investment after multiple calculations. I realized that since starting only most of us have some ideas about investment and liabilities. But we are not able to make many investments because of lack of complete knowledge and fear. This fear is a huge block in the way of being Rich.

When a teacher asks any type of question in a class, than there are many students who knows the right answer, but it is their fear that doesn't allow them to stand up and speak. There are only 1-2 students who do have the courage to stand up and give the answer.

Most of the people are suffering from this rat race as they believe in that studying hard in Academics, getting good grades, getting good job is the only way to success, because it seems to be secure for them. However, they are not aware that this is the riskiest thing they are doing as even a job cannot be permanent and you will be always in this trap for generations. I was also in the same trap and luckily I got this learning in early stage of my life.

These old Ideas are need to be changed, they might have been true for earlier generations but now the society and world has changed a lot. We are living in the era of Information and technology, very soon the AI (Artificial Intelligence) will take over the world which will affect many jobs. Jobs for drivers, mechanics, delivery people are in danger. We need to adapt this change by changing ourselves. The society first needs to UNLEARN and then start learning new things. Our minds should be open to gather as much as knowledge it can. Learning should never stop until you are dead.

Mind is your biggest Asset

There is a very important asset which everyone possesses. We just need to know how to use it in an effective way and in the right direction. Our minds should be trained and get the knowledge of Finances which is the most important of our life. Even though you are a doctor or an engineer, if you are not able to manage your finances than there is no point of working in a high profile job. The financial education is never been taught in school. The school can teach you skills to be a doctor, professor, engineer or an accountant but it cannot teach you how to be Rich. The way to learn is either using self-help books or online learning. Nowadays, there are many seminars and lectures being taught by the most successful people in their life for being financially independent. We should attend those too.

> **"The more that you read, the more things you will know, the more that you learn, the more places you'll go."**
>
> -**Dr Seuss**

Rich people generate money, they never work for money. The only mantra they have is that they know how to put money to earn for them. Money is an employee which never takes leave, never stops working. It works for 24*7. Investments in stocks, bonds, real estate are the things which grow 24 by 7. Not every stock or investment is in profit but yes, if you do not put all your eggs in one basket and calculate the risk than surely you will be in a win-win situation. In these fields, the patience is something which can get you ultimate wealth. Investment in these fields should be made for longer term. Short term investments are not fruitful every time.

Another thing which Rich people do is that they look for opportunities which everyone else has missed. They always think of doing something out of the box. Oyo has born because of the opportunity taken by Ritesh Aggarwal. He did something which everyone else has missed to do.

Rich people keep their surroundings consist of smart people who are even smarter than them because they always teach lessons and gives the best advice. They hire people smarter than them. Smart advisors, smart brokers, smart managers are the key to success. They create their own luck and do smart things keeping their Egos aside.

Learning is an Asset to be Rich

As mentioned earlier, learning is something which keeps you above all the time. It is being proven by every Rich person that their core of success is learning. Learning is not only whatever is being taught in school or Academics. One can learn from anywhere, learning from experiences, making mistakes, learning from society and surroundings, learning from other people's mistakes is the best source of it. Sometimes a person who is much below in terms of status, money or of any age group can give the most vital lesson of life.

Story of two young gentlemen.

When I was studying in Bangalore, before I dropped out of college. I was staying in a PG, where we had two young gentlemen used to work as cleaners. One of them was 15 and other was about to be 14. Those two guys were very hard working. They used to get up early and sleep late at night. One day, when I was in a deep conversation with them. They were telling me about the issues they are facing and what are the reasons because of which they have to work here as cleaners, staying a lot far away from their homes. When they have started telling about the financial issues their family must be facing in their village, I was really shocked. As they never seem to be like they must be facing such issues. They always use to look quite happy and always having a smile on their faces. They taught me the most important lesson in my life.

They said "If you have a problem and you do have a solution to it, then why worry and if you have a problem but there is no possible solution to it, and then also why worry. Time is the biggest healer of everything."

This lesson blew my mind. I was never thinking that way and most of the times used to take so much stress for a small thing. From that day I have started trying my best not to overthink and take so much of stress in my life. Everything goes by time. Nothing is permanent, problems will come and go. Just go with the flow.

This has also taught me one more thing, "Never judge a book by its cover". These people never looked or felt that they must be facing such huge struggles in their life. Anyone can teach you anything which might prove to be the very important lesson in your life.

Rich people work for learning not for money.

When I have started my career again with the small manufacturing unit, I failed drastically. It generated the biggest fear in me for doing or investing in business. I took the same track of working for someone else which seemed to be more safe and secure. It actually did work for couple of years. I was able to earn every month. However, when time passed, I have realized that it is not actually as safe as it seems. Because of the huge loss in my business, I got scared of making sales and getting failures or getting NOs. I though sales are something which is not my cup of tea. I have chosen a field which seemed to be more secure of customer relations, coordination and recruitment but never sales. After, I have started reading; I got to know that the core of being Rich in any business is to make sales. If there are no sales, no revenue can be generated. Very soon, I was able to make up my mind that if I want to get more money, than making sales is a key skill which I need to learn.

But only getting that theoretical knowledge of sale does not mean that you will be able to make sale in the first attempt. Learning to do a sale is like learning to drive a car, even though if you know everything about a car and driving. You still cannot drive a car until you actually try it and practice it. You need to learn it practically. So as like sales, you can only be able to make a sale once you keep on doing it. Every customer is different, with a different way of thinking, different questions and queries, different answers. The only way to master sales is to keep doing it, getting NOs, facing customers.

> "Develop a passion for learning. If you do, you will never cease to grow."
>
> -Anthony J. D'Angelo

Very soon, I have found a new job in sales. When I have started my job, I failed to make any sale in the first month. However, I did give it sometime and started observing and learning from my fellow mates, started listening to their calls and I was able to find the things where I was lacking behind in terms of understanding the mindset of a customer, pitching the product and many more. And Bingo I did my first sale and from then I didn't look back. I started being on top and being the best performer in my team with the most number of sales as my experience with customer relations helped me a lot. I was able to relate both of the fields of sales and customer relations. This has pumped me up with the confidence and I did realize that if you actually want to do something then nothing can stop you to make it.

That is how Rich people do, they learn while working, they are not afraid of getting failures which makes them more confident about taking Risks.

However, to run business, sales is not the only thing you should be able to do. You should have a little understanding and knowledge of every department. So that no one should be able to fool you.

You need to not to master everything to be Rich except your patience and being calm while facing challenges. However, some knowledge about sales, marketing, recruiting new people, management are the needed things. So, never stop learning. People with Rich mentality always keep learning new things about business and life. They always observe the world and society which really helps being an Entrepreneur or a businessman. If you are afraid of doing anything in terms of business, start doing that get failures and continue. The more failures you get the stronger you will be. You just need to have patience. Give it sometime and one day you will be able to make it.

Notes:

4.

Get Through Challenges

The major challenge which everyone gets in their life before starting anything big is to overcome fear. Most of the people around you are there to criticize you. Whenever, you will try to do something, they are always there to screw you and demoralize you. They do that because they were not able to achieve anything. Whenever they tried to do something, they got failed and after sometime they quit. Only few will be there except your parents will support you. So, now it's up to you whom you listen to.

I have never seen any person in my life who never had an accident while learning to drive a Car or Ride a bike. But after some drops you get up and keep practicing it until you actually start driving.

So never give up. It will only demoralize and stop you from trying any new thing. Never say I cannot do it because it will shut the doors of your mind and never let you even try it. Always say how can I do it, it will automatically open the door for new ideas and opportunities for you to get it done.

Whenever, you want to get something, think of the ways how you can get it. Do some research on the people who already have it. Learn from their experiences, start working on it and one day you will hit the bull's eye.

Let me tell you, if you actually want to achieve something, try this-

1. Never tell anyone what you want. Keep it secret to yourself.
2. Never seek for an advice from your relatives, friends or neighborhoods.
3. Start researching about it on your own. You do have the access to Internet where you can explore about anything.
4. Start working on it secretly.
5. In this way, suppose if you fail, nobody will be there to criticize you. Check for things which might have gone wrong and start working on them. But never give up.
6. Never tell your plans to anyone.

Managing your Expenditure

Whenever you earn some amount, you always think of paying others first. You always think of paying your bills, EMIs, loans first which is a wrong practice. Because after that you would have to survive on whatever is left.

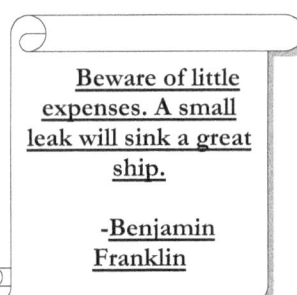

Beware of little expenses. A small leak will sink a great ship.

-Benjamin Franklin

The right way of doing it is to pay yourself first which doesn't mean that you start making unnecessary expenses without paying your bills. You just need to pay yourself first for your essential need, investments etc. and then start paying others. This will generate a pressure on your mind which will let you think to earn more. Most of us do pay other first to remove pressure. But human nature does actually work better under pressure. I am not saying take pressure and get into depression. Take that pressure and open more opportunities for you to earn more. But never start earning from short or easy ways. Don't go into wrong direction. Always choose the right way which may have some obstacles but once you overcome them than the success you will get will stay for a longer period of time. Overnight success will leave you overnight with more loss and guilty.

Notes:

5.

Initial Steps to Success

Results you Want

Whenever you think of starting something, think of the results in both ways positive and negative.

Let's understand it with an example, suppose if a person wants to be cricketer, then once he will become a cricketer, he will have the fame, wealth and he will become a VIP personality. However, if he actually wants all this badly he has to be a devotee in cricket. He has to shut down all the other things in his life. Movies, Netflix, indulgence, chilling out etc. have to be sacrificed for a while. He would have to give all his time in practicing and playing cricket. So now, he should think if he is ready to do all this to achieve his goal. If he is ready to do all this, he should have a strong mentality so that no one else should be able to demotivate him. There will be many obstacles in terms of failures, injuries will come in his way which he has to overcome and keep running on his way to be the cricketer. If he won't give up than he will surely be a great cricketer one day.

So whenever, you want to do something, think of the results you want and how important are those results to you.

The first step to success is to make up your mind and make strong mentality. Think about the results you want and how important these results are for your life.

Make right choices

Every Morning when you wake up, think in your mind, if you really want to move out from the rat race. Choose and select the right path in the direction of your success. If you want to be Rich, choose your spending, select the right thing to purchase. You can choose to spend on liabilities or assets. Think before you save that if you are saving for a liability or an asset. You can choose to save either for buying a car or to invest in an asset like Gold or Business.

> "Nothing is more difficult, and therefore more precious, than to be able to decide."
> -Napoleon Bonaparte

When I have started applying these things, I did immediately cut off my unnecessary expenses, no more spending money on a phone, no more holidays for some time until I have enough assets to pay for them. I have started investing in Gold, stocks, mutual funds and other government schemes. This has changed everything in my life. The lifestyle or daily routine has been changed in my family and we are living in a new life of being more confident about our finances.

So always think every day that where you will be spending your income. Either you want to be in debt or you want to be free financially.

Limit your surroundings

A large group of friends can be good if you want to be in the same life. However, if you want to change your life, you need to change your surroundings. When I got married, I have seen that being with my friends was not good anymore as my family needed me the most. So, I have decided to be with my family and started giving the most of my personal time to

> I believe your atmosphere and your surroundings create a mind state for you.
>
> -Theophilus London

them. This all depends on your priorities, if your family is more important to you, give them your most valuable time. Moreover, the unnecessary friends who you think will always be with you will leave you very soon whenever you will be in a tough situation in your life. The real friend and people can only be recognized when you have nothing and your life is full of difficulties. Than the people who will be with in your toughest times will be your real friends. The friends or relatives who are not real will never let you grow up. They will always be there to pull you down whenever you will grow up a little.

You can check them too if you want to. You can try this to see who all your good friends are.

Today, when you will meet your friends, tell them that you want to start a business. Any type of business you feel like. I can guarantee you that most of them will give you so many reasons of not starting it. They will tell you about their experiences when they failed to do it or someone in their known failed. Only few of them will encourage you or support you with anything good you want to do. So, choose your company wisely.

Learning Should Never Stop

As mentioned earlier, learning is the key to success. And learning in a right direction can do wonders in your life. Choose your Niche which you are passionate about and start learning about it from wherever you want. You can learn from books, videos, internet and much more. We all have different mindset based on our experiences in our life. We all have got different life, different parents, society, experiences, Education. However, there are some common things which are based in our subconscious minds. Those things are being taught to us by our parents, teachers and society. We believe in to be secure and take minimal risks in our life.

Especially people who have the middle class mentality. We all have been taught to work with fixed and secured incomes. Plan our expenses according to the incomes and not taking any risk. These things work fine if you want to live a mediocre life. However, if you want to be Rich, you need to unlearn these lessons and start taking lessons on how to be Rich. I understand that there is no specific mantra or course which can make you Rich in a short period of time. But as soon as you start learning and exploring about it, you will start moving in right direction. Read self-help books, biographies of all Rich and successful people whom you admire the most. Get knowledge every day and start applying it in your life.

Invest in yourself

When I was struggling with my mediocre mentality, I never thought of spending money to learn after my college. However, when I did start exploring, I got to know that if you want to be Rich and successful, you need to start investing in your learning. Start taking financial courses, attend business seminars, buy some self-help business books, and Increase your knowledge by any means. Pay yourself first, as mentioned earlier it creates a positive pressure to earn more to pay your bills, debts, or any other expenses. Again it does not mean that you get into a debt and doesn't pay your bills on time. Start by making small changes to your finances.

> "Self-awareness allows you to self-correct."
> -Bill Hybels

If you really want to buy luxury, create an asset first to pay for it. You want to buy a car or fancy watch or a smart phone, just think that how you can generate a side income apart from your active income source to buy them. This is called as passive income. One should have more than 3 source of income at least.

If you are running a business, choose your brokers and advisors wisely and pay them well. These are the people who work for you to make you Rich. So try to keep them happy as much as possible to get the best piece of advice.

Get a Mentor

When you want to achieve something, look for someone who has already achieved it and learn from his/her experiences. Research about them, read about those people. See what all they have done and faced while achieving the Goal. There can be more than 1 person whom you admire and get inspiration from. Follow the same pattern, learn from their mistakes. Unlike children, they have their heroes whom they admire and like the most, as they always want to be like them. You should also have someone, whom you can learn from and get inspired.

"A mentor is someone who allows you to see the hope inside yourself."
-Oprah Winfrey

My inspiration comes from one of my Uncle, who has lost everything a couple of years back. However, he started all over again, did a lot of hard work, and established a marketing company in just couple of years from nothing but a desire to achieve something. He started working in a full time job for his family's survival. And after sometime he started working on this project too. Even after many failures and facing many obstacles, he never gave up and at last achieved everything he wanted to. I always admire him and he is the main source of my inspiration. Whenever, I feel low about getting any kind of failure or issue I think about him and it motivates me a lot to not give up.

Final Pointers

1. The very first step to be Rich is to make up your mind completely to be the one. Make your mind to face failures, obstacles and challenges.
2. Make a list of the reasons for why you want to be Rich.
3. Reasons like
   a. By being Rich, I want to be free in my life. Free from stress, free from lack of money, free from working for someone else.
   b. I want to live my life as I want to live. Not according to someone else I work for.
   c. I do not want to be in the same rat race for my entire life which every person with middle class mentality is running in.
4. Do make choices every day. Choose to Invest in yourself. Choose your surroundings and friends wisely.
5. Start learning every day, learning should never be stopped. Observe the world and society. Get away from negative people and start searching about successful people and their journey of being successful.
6. Pay yourself first, be in a positive pressure to search for new opportunities of earning.

7. Choose your advisors, brokers wisely and pay them well as they are the people working to make you Rich. So keeping them happy is the most important part if you are running a business.

8. Use assets to buy luxuries. If you want to buy a car, create an asset to pay for it apart from your active Income. Create at least 3-4 source of income in your life.

9. Have a Mentor whom you admire the most. Whom you get inspired and motivate. Research about them.

10. Whatever, you learn start sharing your learning with others. It is always important to discuss your points with someone smarter than you. You will get to know more of it. When you discuss, your knowledge gets increases as there will always be some things missed about that topic which you were not able to get from your source of knowledge. The more you discuss, the more you get.

Notes:

<u>Part-2</u>

<u>Mindset Changed?</u>

<u>Let's Start.</u>

<u>Here in this part, we will take a deep dive into how to start and manage your business.</u>

1.

Introduction to Business

Now, that your mindset has been changed, what next?

How to go about starting your business?

Let's understand, what is the business all about? When you think of starting a business? First think you want to know is in which field or niche you want to start it. To get this, we need to understand what is the purpose of doing business, Money or Wealth? That can be two reasons of doing it until unless you are thinking of yourself. However, the purpose of business should not only be earning. When you look at all big organizations, they are all producing and providing things or services which are helping their customers in providing the ease, status and solutions to their life. The business which is making the life of people easy and providing them a status to stand in front of two people is a 100% successful business. When you start providing value to the people's life, you start getting ultimate returns.

Let's understand this in Detail.

Value Creation

When you think of doing a business, think how you can provide value to the life of your customers. The best product or service is what provides the value to their life in terms of comfort, status and much more. When you start offering things or services which make the life of people effortless, Bingo you hit the bull's eye.

Parts of Every Business

Let's have a look on some major points of a business.

1. Recognizing the need of the people or what is the thing or service you can provide people to make their life better.
2. Now as you have created something, you need to make people aware about it by doing relevant marketing. Create demand of your product in the market.
3. After marketing, you will have a pipeline of interested customers, start providing them services and close as many sales as you can. Turn those interested customers into paying customers.

> **You don't get paid for the hour. You get paid for the value you bring to the hour.**
> -Jim Rohn

4. Deliver the services and products, the way you have promised to deliver. Build trust of your customers for future references.
5. You need to start managing your finances and see if you are making enough to run the business further.

Let me take an example to make it more clearly for you.

Suppose if you are thinking of starting a business of Paper Cups. Nowadays, the paper cups are huge in demand as they are ecofriendly and can be thrown after using them once. Most of the Juice shop owners and party organizers are using them. Now as there is a huge demand in the market of it. You have got the value of the product as people need this product and there is a huge demand of it in the market to the business owners and for personal use too.

Start building the product with a small manufacturing unit and meanwhile start doing marketing of it to get the pipeline of the interested customers. You can do door to door marketing, can get templates printed, distribute them in the relevant market and can do social media marketing too. You can also put them on Online Selling websites such as Amazon, Flipkart etc. You can sell them   to the wholesale sellers and to the retails shops to at the price with highest profit margin which the customers can bear and you need to check the competitors price too which you can do by start purchasing them from your competitors.

When you have got the pipeline of the interested customers, start delivering the product to them with good packaging and minimal damage. As soon as you start delivering the product, the revenue will be generated.

Calculate your cost of production and start managing your expenses accordingly, try to reach as many customers as you can. This is a business which will build clientage and the business will run in continuation as per the demand in the market. You can get as many clients as you can. Moreover, you can provide the facility of customizing the paper cups according to the requirements of your clients in terms of size and design.

And Bingo, you have a business to run.

These are the basic steps and a basic scenario you need to understand and keep in mind while thinking of doing a business. However, there are many more things we need to learn about these basic steps by diving deep into it.

<u>Notes:</u>

2.

Examining a Business before you Start.

Now that you have understood about the basic scenario of a business, let me take you into the detail of examining a business before you start.

Skills Should Have Economic Values.

Suppose you have a skill of typing fast and accurate. However, this is the skills which a normal person doesn't bother about much to pay you to learn it. Nowadays, everybody has computers and laptops at their homes and everybody is more than average in typing. There are many online free apps to make your typing fast. So this skill can be good for you however, not good for doing a business of it. The skills you possess should have good economic value in the market.

This is like being a great graphic designer or video editor. In this era of internet and reels, everybody wants to learn video editing and everybody wants to have a good graphic designer. They are eager to pay a professional to get these services.

Hard Rule of Market

Market and people always looks for something which is more reliable, easily accessible and lower in price.

Suppose, if you create a car which works on solar energy and cost of production is also very high for it. Now think, this car will need solar energy to run which can only be provided in daytime and in Night it won't work. Although it will save fuel cost and will be ecofriendly. Most of the people will not buy it as the car is something which needs to work as soon as we need it. Nobody will pay a high cost to buy a car which will not work at night or in a cloudy area or at a place where the sun light is not available.

People want something which is easy to use and can be used whenever is needed. They are more likely to pay for a car works on fuel or electricity, as these two things are available 24*7.

Rather than creating such car, you can create something like an electric vehicle.

Understanding What People Actually Want.

There is a huge psychology works behind running a business and making a successful business. You need to analyze the needs and wants of the people.

It is being mentioned by Josh Kaufman in his "The Personal MBA". He tells about the theory of Abraham Maslow, the progress of people goes through five stages which are physiology, safety, belonging/love, esteem and self-actualization. Where the order starts from physiology and goes up to self-actualization.

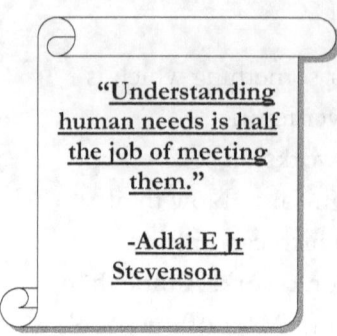

"Understanding human needs is half the job of meeting them."

-Adlai E Jr Stevenson

It means if someone is physically ill than the person is less likely to think or concentrate about how what people think about that person. The first preference of an ill person is always to get healthy as soon as possible.

So, if you are dealing with fancy watches which are starting from above 10,000 Rupees. Than a person who is struggling to fulfil his basic needs will not care about your watches and won't even listen to your offer at all.

Another thing to consider is social status which is somewhat not as important as survival. However, nowadays most of the people are not that much struggling to get food, shelter or clothing which are the essential needs for survival. Their prime focus is going on their social status. They are doing a lot of hard work to get a good social status to stand in a high profile group of people. Whenever, you have something to offer people will think that how the product or service you are offering will affect their social status. So whenever you think of starting a business, analyze that how your product or service will affect their social status.

Market Evaluation

When you think of evaluating the market of a particular product or service, there are some major points you should consider.

1. First thing you should check that how eager are people about to get the same kind of product you are

offering. Nobody will bother about getting an old movie DVD, the first show of a newly released movie will have huge demand.

2. How big is the market of the product? Which you are offering is the another important thing to consider. Nowadays, the market of an Alarm clock is not as big as it is being overtaken by cell phones, same thing in terms of Calculator and Tape Recorder. However, market of Android and IOS phones are huge.

3. Provide a service or product in a price which worth to it. Getting a pack of potato chips can be as less as 10 Rupees per unit however, a car can cost you lakhs of rupees. It all depends on the value of product. Always, decide the product according to the value it is providing to your customers.

> "Innovation needs to be part of your culture. Customers are transforming faster than we are, and if we don't catch up, we're in trouble."
>
> -Ian Schafer

4. Check how much it will cost you in Marketing. How much cost and effort it will take to have a new paying customer. Having a restaurant on a highway doesn't need much marketing. However, a new movie will require a huge amount of capital to do marketing and promotions.

5. How much the production and delivery of your product or service will cost you. Being a trainer you won't require much investment, building a

manufacturing unit can cost lakhs or crores of rupees to set up.

6. How unique your product or services are from the ones which are already available in the market. There are multiple android phones are available in the market but IOS is only being provided by one company.

7. How fast you can create or manufacture your product. Producing candies is much faster than manufacturing a car.

8. You also need to calculate the cost of starting a business. Opening a grocery shop will not require much capital however, a manufacturing plant will cost you a lot.

9. One more thing you should check is that, how much effort you need to put after the first sale is made. The consulting business will require the same ongoing efforts to continue the business, writing a book will only require a one-time effort and can be sold on and on.

Competition

There is a huge possibility that whatever service or product you want to provide, is already being provided in the market until you invent something new. So, now the question comes up that how will you cope up with the competition.

The best way to check what your competitors are offering is to actually buy their product or service. Be their customer and analyze how they are surviving in the market. Check their prices, offers, delivery, quality, reliability of their product. Provide the better quality and offers in a lesser price if possible to get ahead.

> **"Competition is not about tearing others down, but about building yourself up."**
>
> **-Jennifer Lynn Barnes**

Suppose you want to open a digital marketing agency. There are multiple marketing agencies are there in the market which are huge. Pick some of the best companies and buy their services. See what are they providing in what price. What kind of packages they have, what are the services they are not providing which you can offer?

Do proper analysis and then start your own business, it is not like that your business will work 100% but after all these calculations and analysis, you will have less chances of failure. Business is something which can only be run when you learn from failures. You cannot do business until unless you actually do it. Only theoretical knowledge about it won't be enough to hit it.

<u>Notes:</u>

3.

Types of Business

There are various types of businesses which can create great value and can be extremely successful. Let's have a look at them one by one.

Business Based on a Product.

1. Whenever you think of a business the first things come up in our mind is a product. There are tons of businesses which are based on a product.
a. If you are thinking of doing a business of a product, then first thing you need to check is the demand of the product in a market.
b. Check what is the minimal cost you can build a product with the best quality.
c. Sell as many units as you can with the maximum profit margin however, the price should worth the quality of the product and should be able to compete in the market.
d. Keep enough stock to fulfil the demand so that the delivery should not be delayed.

Example: Suppose if you are thinking of doing a business of shirt manufacturing. There are two things you can do either you can do manufacturing of it and sell them to other wholesalers and retailers. Or you can sell it with your name, creating your own brand.

In both the things you need to keep in mind that shirt manufacturing is a business which is already in the market since years and there are a lot of people who are already doing it. The demand will always be there for it as it is an essential product. So the first point is clear that the demand is there.

Check the minimum cost of production with best quality. Where there are many shirts which are of low price with average quality and goes on with better quality and higher prices. If you are going for an average quality shirt, then the profit of margin will be low so to grow up, you need to make more sales.

However, when you give the best quality, the cost of production will be high and the profit of margin will also be good. So even though if the number of sales will be low but those sales can give you good profit. There are again some circumstances comes up when you deliver quality, you need to build trust for your product in the market and has to spend on marketing too.

Business based on Services

Another type of business which is in the market from a very long time is providing a service in exchange of money.

Service is helping or assisting people and charge them for each service.

While doing such type of business, let's see what are the things need to be considered.

1. Hire skilful people to provide the best of the services which customers require.
2. Never compromise with quality.
3. Gain customers, build trust and keep providing the better services to retain them.

Some examples of doing a business of providing the services are Video Editors, Digital Marketers, Barbers and many more.

> **"A business absolutely devoted to service will have only one worry about profits. They will be embarrassingly large"**
>
> -Henry Ford

Suppose if you want to start a digital marketing business. Firstly, you need to have a good knowledge about digital marketing. Even though you are not a professional but there must be enough knowledge you should have to manage and run the business. Hire professionals who can work efficiently. There are different fields in digital marketing, you can either help customers with every type of digital marketing service or your company can choose some of them and provide the best of it. You can provide social media marketing, google ads, SEO, SMO etc. But being specialized in one of them seems more appealing.

Asset that need to be created only once.

There is an another form of business which you can use to earn money which is proved to be the easiest way to earn money. That form of business is called as shared resource. An asset which needs to be created at once for full time earnings is like building a Banquet hall (party halls), Farm Houses, Hotel or even writing a book. Such type of business or sources of income are need to be built only once and they can let you earn by putting them on rent. They will be continuously generating income with small investment on maintaining the asset.

If you want to create a shared resource, there are some things you need to keep in mind.

1. Build an asset people want to have access to.

2. Let the people rent your asset on and on without affecting the quality of it.
3. Charge enough money to run and maintain the asset.
4. Improve the quality of it on regular basis.

Some more examples of shared resource will be GYMs, Fitness Clubs etc. You can purchase the equipment and let the people use these machines in exchange of a monthly charge.

Services on Rent

The most trending business nowadays is of monthly rental services or subscriptions.

Let's understand this in detail, a subscription or service on rent is a program being provided on a continuous basis in exchange of continuous monthly, weekly or yearly charges. This form of business can build clients for you.

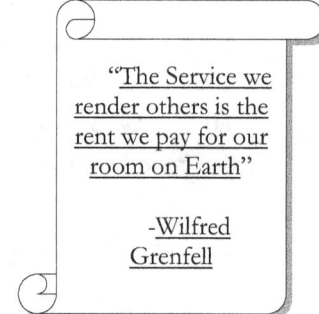

"The Service we render others is the rent we pay for our room on Earth"

-Wilfred Grenfell

If you provide exactly the same which you have promised, then the customers will be loyal to you and continue taking services from you.

We have got many subscription services providers such as Netflix, Hot star, Amazon Prime and much more. However, the eldest subscription is TV service provider. TV services are charging on a monthly basis for the channels they offer. If you do not pay them for a month, they will stop providing you the service. Same scenario works with Internet Service Providers.

Some points to remember, before looking to start such business.

1. You need to provide a significant service on a regular basis.
2. Build a client base and get new subscribers by reaching them on regular basis. This will compensate those subscribers which might discontinue your services for any specific reason.
3. Charge customers on monthly basis for the service you are providing.
4. Try to retain your subscribers for as long as possible.

If you take care of these things, you can build a great business. This subscription can work in any type of services you provide if you know how to maintain that. A barber can also offer a subscription and can offer some services in a package on monthly basis to his loyal customers and can charge them on timely basis.

Retail business.

Another usual form of business is a retail or reselling business. In this business you can buy product to keep an Inventory and sell them further to individual customers with a good profit margin which market can bear.

> "The only thing worse than starting something and failing is not starting something."
>
> -Seth Godin

Suppose, think of a business of packaged food products, the manufacturer cannot sell it to individual customers directly as it won't be time efficient. Instead, he can sell products to whole sellers or retailers in bulk quantity and focus on manufacturing more units. Then the whole sellers and retailers will further sell their products to individual customers by keeping an acceptable profit margin.

Points to remember:

1. Have enough money to Invest and buy products in bulk to keep a good inventory on as low price as possible.
2. Take care of your inventory and products, secure them from being damaged before they get sold out.
3. Reach as many customers as you can to find the potential ones, so that the business can run and it will also be secured for products from being damaged.
4. Set a high profit margin which is acceptable by the customers to generate profit.

This business does not require rocket science, a normal person with good sense of business can easily do it.

Lease

Here is a form of business, which does not require much efforts but might require a good investment.

Lease is a process where you get an asset which society want to use, however not everyone is able to buy it. You can provide that asset to the customers who are in need on lease for specific period of time to them in exchange of some amount.

As an example, you can have a business of restaurant or hotels, which you do not want to run on your own and can lease that to a potential business person who want to start business of a restaurant or hotel however, cannot build it. You can provide them your hotel for a year or any specific period of time to run the business and charge them for a lease. Get an agreement on which both parties can agree.

There are some major points to remember.

1. Buy something which is in demand.
2. Provide the asset to a potential business person by signing a mutual agreement.
3. Keep a security amount to protect yourself from the damage being done by the other party while your asset was on lease. So that you do not have to bear the damage.
4. This form of business can make millions for you if you have a good amount to invest.

Agency

This is something where you do not require much investment but might require good knowledge and efforts.

In this business, you do not need to actually buy the product or an asset. You do not need to actually buy the product or an asset. You can deal with the sellers or companies where you can do marketing and sales for them and charges some amount as a commission. You can get potential customers for them.

Some examples of such businesses are BPOs, Job Consultancies, Online selling platforms like Amazon, flipkart, Meesho etc.

Let's take an example and understand this in detail. A business of job consultancy can be a good example for such business. Where you can deal with the organizations where they require candidates on timely basis and have a huge demand. You can do marketing of their jobs and get some potential candidates, filter those candidates for them according to their job requirements and get them interviewed. Once these candidates join the company, you can charge them per candidate.

There are some things to remember:

1. Look for organizations which are offering valuable asset.
2. Build your pipeline of potential customers and build their trust who are ready to buy it from you.
3. Get an agreement with mutual terms and conditions of both the parties.
4. Take good commission, which is acceptable by the organization.

These business are running on a high level and are in demand nowadays.

Gathering people of same interests.

Think, you know certain amount of people who has same point of interests in something. Which means all of them are in interested in same type of things or content and you give them what they are interested in. That is how you can make money by advertising the products or services of their interest. In exchange of the advertising you can charge the product or service provider as it will literally increase their sales.

> Once social media was introduced, it enabled a new way for people, particularly the younger generation, to connect with one another, based on common interests, goals and even values.
>
> -Raymond Arroyo

Let me give you an example: - Nowadays content creators are earning a lot through this type of business. They have audience with specific type of interest in their content and they have a great chance to provide them the services or products they are looking for. You need to make sure that advertising should not go to the extent where the audience you have start losing interest in your content as many people don't like to watch much advertising. Remember, they are your audience because they are more interested in your original content and not the advertising.

You need to remember some major points when you think of doing something like this:
1. Identify the interests of a specific audience.
2. Create and maintain the attention of your audience before you lose them.
3. Find the organizations and companies who are ready to pay you for advertising their product or service. Make sure you never do false advertising.

Offering Loan by charging pre-defined interest rate.

As we have learnt in earlier phase of this book, Rich people let their money work for them. Here is a direct form of business which can make you money using you own money. Giving a specific amount to a person who is in urgent need of it and get it repaid on monthly, quarterly or yearly basis with pre-defined rate of interest. However, this could be risky. Not everyone in this world is good enough to repay you.

Earning through this method can be risky and tricky.

Take care of below points before doing such business:

1. Firstly, you need to have enough amount of money to lend as most of the people look for higher amounts.
2. Look for people who are in need of money, also check their background status to see if they will be able to repay you in future.
3. Set an interest rate which is acceptable by both the parties.
4. Check the probability that how many people seems to be suspicious who might not be able to you or intentionally don't want to pay you back. Avoid losses by taking some security as a collateral.

Loan can be of different types depending upon the need of a person. Vehicle loan, Home loan, personal loan etc. All these can have different time period of repayments with different rate of interests. Credit cards are an another form of providing loan. Where a card holder can make the payment for anything without actually paying for it right away. The card holder will have to repay the amount to bank or card issuer company after some period of time with a rate of interest.

Offering a Right to someone in exchange of money.

This form of business is like all around us. However, a bit underrated or we can't see it directly. Providing a right to potential customers to take a specific action in future if they want to, giving them a deadline of taking that action.

Let's understand this is in detail:

Suppose you want to attend a concert which is happening next month. However, you are not sure about attending it. So, you can buy a ticket and reserve your place in the concert which will be a security that even if all the seats are booked, you won't have to worry.

Now it is up to you that if you will actually be able to attend it according to your priorities. You have got a right on that particular seat whether you will attend it or not.

This is how this business works, offering a right to potential customers for a specific period of time and charging them a specific amount of it.

Another example of such business will be booking an apartment or hotel for future. Where you can pay deposit amount to reserve your room or apartment and when the time comes up you have the right to decide whether you want to move in or not.

Points to Remember:

1. Firstly, you need to identify that what are the actions which your potential customers would be interested in.

2. Provide them the right to take action until a specific time period.

3. You need to convince them that the amount you are charging is worth taking a risk of reserving your right to take action in future which you are not 100% sure off.

4. Give them a deadline to take that action. After the deadline the validity should get expire of the specific ticket or booking.

Providing Insurance and Safety Cover.

Here is another trending business which is providing value to people. Insurances are now a necessity of people and are huge in demand.

First, we need to understand what Insurance is:

How will it feel when you will be able to transfer your risk on someone else in exchange of some recurring charge to be paid over a specific period of time? This is where Insurance comes up.
Here, the insurance provider will take the risk of your things, health and your life. And will be available to help you in terms of money in your tough times. When you go under any losses in terms of health, thing or even life.

> **To sell Insurances, you just need to check, how many dependents are there on the paying person.**

In current times, it is being very competitive to start a business of Insurance. Still there is a huge market waiting for you to come up and take their Risk.

Insurance can be of a thing, majorly a vehicle, where you can transfer a Risk of it being damaged and bear the maintenance cost. Where you will pay a specific amount to get your car insured. And if any miss-happening happens than the insurance provider will bear the cost of it. Luckily, if there will be no damage happens to your car than the insurance provider will keep the amount paid.

Same scenario works with health insurance and in case of life insurance, by any chance if you die than your family left behind will get some specific amount of money according to the plan you have chosen.

There are certain terms and conditions which you need to put while taking risks of others.

Points to remember:

1. While starting such business, you need to go through all the legal formalities needed. You need to get a legal agreement where you and policy holder can agree on some terms and conditions.
2. You also need to estimate the amount of risk which you will be transferring from policy holder to you.
3. Take a fixed amount of timely basis as premium.
4. Analyse the loss of policy holder, when needed to pass the claim. Check if the loss happened is under terms and conditions you have agreed on.

Investing in Other Businesses

Here is the form of business which is very popular amongst the business men who are risk loving as this can be a bit tricky or risky to win this business. In such type of business, a person who has good knowledge about how a business works, can invest capital to the start-ups or existing companies to help them in expanding in the market. This investment can help you in earning without actually running the business. Here, you just make investment in other companies in exchange of equity, stocks or certain amount of profit. Angel Investing, Venture Capital and investing in stocks are the direct examples of such type of businesses. However, it is not that easy as throwing money anywhere. This can lead to gambling instead of investing. You should have certain experience and knowledge about business to see if the company will be able to exist in the market and make enough profit.

To do such investments, go through some points mentioned below:

1. First of all, you need to have enough resources or capital to invest. A couple of lakh rupees won't be much to invest in an organization. Still there will be some start-ups you might find to invest in.

2. Look for business or start-up which you can be sure off that it will work in the market and worth investing in it. A business with large investment will have a same amount of Risk.

3. Check the current worth of the business and see how much it can go up to in the future. What will be the probability of the business to go in loss in future.

4. After checking all these things, negotiate with the owner for the profit and ownership percentage to earn enough worth investing the required capital.

5. Once you are sure of all the points above, you will have a good amount of assets to earn for you without actually working in it.

Notes:

4.

Major Strategies to run a business.

Now, that as we have learnt about different types of businesses. Let's have a look on some strategies which can really help while you are thinking of starting a business. We will look on these strategies one by one.

1. _Removing hassle in exchange of charge._

When people were not able to communicate, telephones were invented, when people were not able to travel efficiently, motor cars born, when people were not able to see in dark, bulb invented. All these things invented when people wanted to have solution to their problems and hassles. As mentioned earlier, business or entrepreneurship is only a solution to a hassle or a problem which those business owners were able to identify and provide the

To have a successful business, identify a common problem and solve it in exchange of charge.

solution. If you identify an issue in almost everyone's life and are able to provide a solution, BINGO this is what you are looking for to do.

Problems can be of any type; some basic hassles or problems are listed below:

1. Anything which is taking a lot of time to complete can be a good opportunity for you to look for some solution which can reduce the time of completing a particular task. Once you have the solution, offer it to the society in exchange of charge.

2. Things or tasks which require a lot of efforts physically or mentally to complete is again an opportunity to find a solution which can reduce the effort.

3. Tasks which involves a lot of confusion, uncertainty or complexity is a hassle which you can think of that what you can do to make it simple and present it to those who are facing same issues.

4. If you have something which can be cost efficient than the one which is already existing in the market can be a good solution. Take an example of internet, it used to be very costly until Reliance Jio was born.

5. Things or tasks which require specialization and experience to complete can be costly as you would need to hire someone to do it for you. However, if you are able to provide something or a device which anyone can use will be a good solution to this problem.

Value worth paying for it.

If you are able to identify any specific problem in the society which you can fix, then you have a great opportunity to start a business. However, you need to analyse that how much hassle is there in doing a task or using a thing and how much a person will be willing to pay for your solution. No one would like to pay thousands of rupees to travel with in a city in a normal car until one is willing to travel in a luxury car. As it is not only benefits as travelling but also provides social status. So, analyse how much one will be able to pay for the value you are providing.

The most offers which are worth paying for it will always fulfil one or more needs or requirements of a person. You need to present your offer in such a way that customer should be able to visualize the end results of using your service or product. Your service or product should also be able to provide a good status to your customer, as this is what is the essential need of everyone along with a solution to a problem.

Offering Value in different forms.

We have learnt multiple types of businesses earlier. It is not like that you can only do one of the business from them. The smart action will be to offer multiple forms of values along with your product or service.

Let's understand this by taking an example: -

DishTV, Tataplay or any other TV service providers are offering TV services majorly, along with that

> **"If you are not taking care of your customer, your competitor will"**
> -Bob Hooey

they offer subscriptions for multiple OTT platforms like Netflix, Amazon Prime, Hotstar and much more. They are not only limited to TV services, some of them do provide Internet services too. Here, a customer will be able to choose what all services they want to avail. Similarly, take an example of swiggy. It has started as online food ordering platform from your favourite restaurants, tied up with some restaurants on its app to book dineout or reserve a table for yourself in your favourite restaurant. Now, they have also started offering groceries which you can get delivered to your door step.

This how a business can provide different forms of value to its customers.

Combining different forms of value.

Another thing which you can do make your business more successful is to combine two or more forms of value and make a bundle or package of it. So that it can be easy for a customer to avail them all together. Make it more cost effective by adding attractive offers on such packages. Here, you can understand this better by taking an example of a SIM card provider. A phone company will never offer you a blank SIM card or a basic phone plan. They are not there to only offer you basic calling service. When you buy any of their plan, you not only get

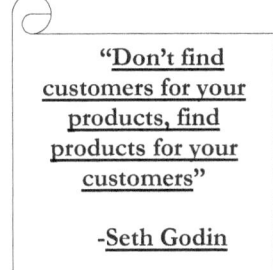

"**Don't find customers for your products, find products for your customers**"

-**Seth Godin**

basic service plan but along with that they provide SMS service, Internet, roaming and much more. This is how they combine more than two forms of value by making packages. This strategy increases the value of your offer and people tent to pay you more as it solves their different communication hassles together.

Another example of it will be: -

Suppose, if you go to buy a car, the car company will not only provide you the car, along with that they get the insurance of your car with some cool accessories and get you some free maintenance services too.

Even then you can do opposite of that too, instead of combining the forms together, you can also provide the value by splitting the forms to those who only need one product or service. This will become more cost efficient for them.

Being a Mediator or removing the one.

Here we are talking about two different scenarios. Let's understand them one by one: -

Being a Mediator: Suppose if you want to buy or invest in something which you are not sure of. Where you do not have the complete knowledge of product, service or market. Here is when a mediator comes into the picture. Where you do not have the complete expertise about a particular field, product, service or market. The expert can give you the best advice of where you should put your money in.

If you are going or planning to study abroad. There is a possibility that you might now aware of many things about the course, university, place or accommodation. So, there are many consulting agencies or companies who have experts to do counselling for you. Who can suggest you the right path and location to go for.

Nowadays, such type of businesses is expanding in the market on a bigger level. Where you can have an expertise in a particular field and can help the society by giving your valuable advice and charge them in exchange of it.

Some more examples of such businesses would be travel consulting, real estate agents, stock brokers, Job consultancies etc. Where I have worked in two of the fields above by being an expert as a job consultant and a Global Property Consultant.

> Mediators do not choose the conflicts they became involved in, but the parties to the conflict choose the mediator. Their participation as intermediaries is based on the trust of all the conflicting parties.
>
> -Martti Ahtisaari

This is how you can build a business by getting an expertise and being a mediator between the customer and the other party to make them right decision and close the deal in exchange of charge or commission.

Removing a Mediator: - This is what, where you can help the society by offering the things and services directly to the customers by removing the mediators in the market. Which will become more cost effective and transparent for customers as the charges which used to be taken by the mediators will be removed.

As an example many E-commerce websites has removed many retailers who used to sell things on higher prices. Now you all have a platform to actually select the product or service you want from a large pool of varieties. Amazon, flipkart are the major examples of it.

Disclose your Idea

Many of us think that if they have a good idea to establish something, they should keep it secret as anyone can steal their idea. I used to have the same mentality until I got this learning. This is not actually happening. It means that sharing your unique idea doesn't mean that It will be stolen. It is always better to discuss your idea with others. When you discuss it, you get even more powerful insights and some supporting ideas as well. Many people will share their experiences with such ideas and it will help you in learning through their experiences and mistakes they might have made.

Suppose, if you are working on manufacturing a product, software or anything else. As soon as you start working on it, put your initial model of your idea to your potential customers, family members or friends. There is a high possibility that you will might receive many negative and demotivating points to no go ahead with that idea further. However, you do not have to focus on those negative points, just try to look why the other person has such negative points for such idea or product. And see how you can make it better.

This will let them give you a feedback, ideas and any good changes should be made. This will help you in making even better product or anything else. Those who don't present the initial model of their product rather they directly offer the final product has the highest possibility that their product will not be able to fulfil the needs of your customers.

So if you have any idea, create a basic initial model or design of it and present it in front of your potential customers to see what better changes of additions can be done to the final product.

Continuous Updates

Once your final product is launched doesn't mean that it is done. According to human psychology, human nature is like a person gets bored of everything after sometime which means they can get bores of your product too very soon. To overcome this, you need to keep on improving your product or services with the necessary changes in your product or services. Updating is very important to present every time a new and better product to your potential customers.

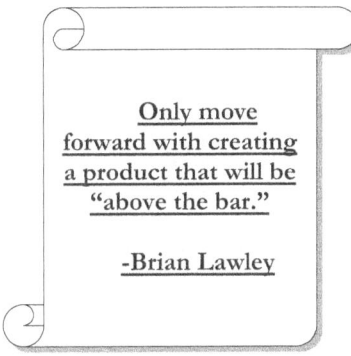

Only move forward with creating a product that will be "above the bar."

-Brian Lawley

Imagine, if you are still using the first Iphone being launched by Apple. What could have been the situation of the company. It is having huge market in smart phones because of continuous updates and improvement in their products. Because company knows that people get bored of using same products after some period of time.

Also, while doing such updates and changes, you need to remember that your new upcoming update should not take very long time to be launched. The faster your launch, the more you have chance of getting new potential customers. Set a specific time line for yourself to launch your updated product according to the expectations of your customers. Analyse the market, see what are the responses you are getting from your potential customers. This can be done by taking continuous feedbacks from your users which is our next topic to learn.

Getting and Applying Feedback

Whenever you build and launch something. There is a high probability that some of your potential customers need to get some changes to be dine on your product to make it better. And considering those feedbacks will be very fruitful for you.

As I am writing this book, there is a huge probability that my readers want to give some feedback about it to make the necessary changes. So I should be open to accept those feedbacks and try to apply most of them in my next upcoming book after analysing all of them.

There are some points to remember while considering feedbacks: -

- When you are seeking feedbacks, make sure to seek your potential customers who don't know you personally. As they will always give you honest points to improve your product. If you only seek feedback from your friends and family, there are high chances that this will not give an honest feedback.

> We all need people who will give us feedback. That's how we improve.
>
> -Bill Gates

- While taking feedbacks, never be argumentative. There are high chances that you won't feel good after getting some negative feedback. However, take it as an opportunity for you to improve your product. While taking feedbacks don't talk much or ask many questions in the conversation. Let your customers speak the most about your product or service. Keep some common and major points that will be worth applying to your product.

- There is one more thing which you can do to get good idea about the market. To analyse that your updated product is good to go, let your potential customers place an order in advance to see their response. If you get good number or order for the product which is yet to launch, then it means you are going in a right direction. However, if the numbers are not good it means you still need to work more on your product.

Expectations before paying for anything.

When you have to purchase something, there are some things you will check before paying for it. A certain product or service should have more value than the money you have in your pocket.

This book might not take much amount of money to printed and published. However, there will be a certain price which a reader needs to pay in exchange of it. Which means this book should provide you more value than the money which you need to lose in exchange of it.

Same way, a potential customer will always consider some points before paying for your product.

1. First thing they will consider is how good your product or service will work?
2. Another thing to be considered will be the time consumption in using your product. The less time it will take to do a task, the more demanding it will be. As everybody wants to get something which is time efficient.
3. A product should work in such a way that owner should be able rely on it.
4. How much efforts do it require to use the product and how many things it can do? If your product can do multiple task and a person don't need to pay for different products to do different task, it will be more appealing.

5. The last thing but not the least is the cost of the
    product. The product should not cost much
    depending on the value it is providing.

These were some basic things which a customer will
consider before paying for your product. Make an offer
which convinces your customer to take out the money
from their pockets. However, not everyone has same
considerations all the time. It will always depend on their
personal priorities too.

Some more points to consider

If you ask someone, that what are their expectations
from your product, there is a guarantee that each and
every one would not want to compromise with anything
or parameter. Everyone want to have something which
provides 100% up to their expectations. So what actually
happens is? They just go with the product which suits the
best of their requirements. You need to offer something
which suits the best of their requirements. A product
which is able to complete multiple requests or tasks at the
minimum period of time efficiently with very low cost
and is reliable will be more fruitful for customers
depending on their priorities. Before launching a product,
take a survey from a potential market asking them about
their priorities, make a list of things and services you can
provide in your upcoming project. Ask them to give
ratings according to their priorities what will they would
like to have the most. Analyse the data and try to add
most of them to your product or services. This is how
you can test your product before building it to minimize
the risk of loss.

Assumptions

Before starting any business, make some assumptions that if you invest a certain amount of capital and efforts, will it work in your favour or not?

Let's take an example:

Suppose if you are a skilled professional and you are thinking of training that skill to people. You must have a pool of possible interested people, who want to learn the same skill. Open your training centre in the area where there are maximum number of potential paying learners who are ready to pay a certain amount to learn the skill.

> Remember, we see the world not as it is but as we are. Most of us see through the eyes of our fears and our limiting beliefs and our false assumptions.
> -Robin S. Sharma

See, how much it will cost you to take a particular place to lease, what will be the monthly expenses for operating it including the systems, employee salaries and maintenance. Assume what will be the least number of trainees you will get in next couple of months. Match that if you will be able to cover up the investment and running cost of it. These assumptions and calculations will give you a fair idea about your upcoming business model. Also consider all the worst case scenarios to see that how much loss you can bear if your assumptions go wrong.

Testing before making it Available

Finally, you have the product which you have built after following all the pointers we have learnt earlier about making investments. Now, should the product be launched finally in that market? No, still before launching a product, do the final testing while using the product on your own Use your product for some time and test it considering all the applicable matrices. To see, if it is up to the mark? There is a possibility you might find some fault or bug in the product or service. Until the issue is fixed, the product shouldn't be launched as it might degrade the reputations of the product and company.

Like most of the car companies do, test your product in front of your potential customers to show them the product they have pre-ordered is up to their expectations. This will help you in gaining their trust and make them feel that the amount they had paid was worth putting in. Also remember, never make them pay before the product is ready to deliver, just take orders prior and you can also ask them to put their payment details in to see how many potential customers you have.

Notes:

5.

Different Segments of Business.

As we had a look on how a business works. Now, we will look at some major parts of business. There are some segments of business which are necessary to study. Let's have a look on them one by one.

1. _Marketing_

Marketing is the process of making yourself visible in front of the pool of your potential customers. If they don't know who you are, what your business is and what you are offering, there will be no way to convert them from potential customers to paying customers. Marketing can be tricky and to make it more efficient you need to consider some major points mentioned below:

Seeking Attention

- The first rule of marketing is to get attention of your potential customers. In this fast moving world, it is very tricky to grab the attention. You need to present your offerings in such a way, that if someone looks at you they should stop and explore what exactly you are offering. Make your advertisement short, crisp and to the point.

Medium

- The another thing which need to be considered is that what you are showing them. Most of your potential customers will ignore whatever you are showing them if that is not of their interest. People only care about the things which they are interested in. Choose your marketing medium wisely. No one wants to read a template being distributed in a public place. As mentioned, they do not have time for that.

Uniqueness

- You may not be able to find a person with normal attire in the crowd of thousand people, a clown can be recognized anywhere. This means you have to do something unique which will be able to grab the attention of people. People tend to give attention to things which are odd.

Right Audience

- A business of kid products won't be able to attract the whole society. As the unmarried youngsters and the elderly people won't care about what you have to offer. Only the recently married people will care about it. So choose the right audience for marketing.

Generate Curiosity

- Grabbing someone's attention means you need to distract their attention from whatever they are thinking now which not an easy task is. Our brains do react to things immediately when we hear or look at something which seems to be either surprising and shocking. You need to show your offerings in such a way which will make your audience curious to know about.

Awareness

"Stopping advertising to save money is like stopping your watch to save time" -Henry Ford

- There are people who are not even aware about the problem which you are solving with your offering, and some of them are aware about the problem, seeking solution to it. So you need to understand and identify that how your marketing strategy should be. You cannot make people interested in your offer without showing them the problem and the person who is already aware about it, won't bother to listen to the problem again through your marketing and might ignore it as he/she doesn't have that much time.

Show End Result

- According to psychology, most people are not actually bothered about knowing all the features of your product and services. Rather they are more interested in knowing about the benefits and end result of your product. Focus more on mentioning the end results of your product while doing marketing.

Showing Demo

- When TATA bought land rover, the company did put a bump in the middle of the street which was really hard to cross for many of the luxurious cars then a range rover arrived and crossed the bump without any hassle. Which showed the major quality of this car which is offloading. The car proved to be best for those who like to do offloading and driving in hilly areas. This shows that demonstration of a product works best in terms of marketing. When you show people what are the major qualities of your product by actually demonstrating, it gives a great impact.

Analyse audience to avoid wasting time.

- In the era of internet and web, it is easy to see that what your probable customers are looking for. Suppose if you are into a business of kid's products. It would be worthless of doing marketing in front of the unmarried youngsters. However, it would be really efficient if you can find who all are expecting to be a parent, which can be done easily filtered out by their searches on web and social media. This is how you see things on internet which are best of your interest.

It is a waste of money and efforts which you put in doing marketing where you try to sell something to your customers which they actually don't want to buy. Offering a product or service which is in their desire will work best for you. Let them get convinced on their own to take money out of their pockets.

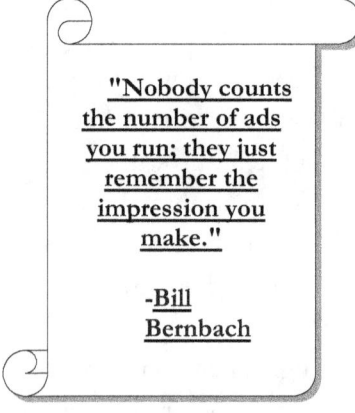

"Nobody counts the number of ads you run; they just remember the impression you make."

-Bill Bernbach

Let your customers try your product.

- When you enter a Croma Store or any other electronic devices store, there is a huge possibility that you will find some exclusive products on table for you to use them and try them. Why is that so? This is because when you actually use any device, you start thinking and feeling that how it would feel if you buy it and will it be worth investing money into it.

Short and Crisp

- It is very hard to describe everything about your product or service while doing marketing. You cannot show every small feature of it. Instead you can show them the major features which suits the best to them. Frame your advertising and the description to minimize it as much as possible.

Offer something for free

- Nowadays, every company especially online streaming sites do offers free subscriptions which attracts most of the customers. Offering something valuable for free always works great at marketing. If you want your customers to actually try your product once. Offer them something for free. Let them try your services and then decide if they want to continue.

Seek Permission

- It is really not worth of interrupting anyone with your marketing whether they are interested in your offer or not. Rather you can seek and ask for permission from those who have taken the value your offered for free. Ask them when you can take a follow up for continuation of your service. This make them feel that they have a control on making the decision to continue with your product or service.

Informative Tag Line

- As your potential customers do not have much time to listen to all the description of your product. Use a tag line or a title to describe the major benefit of your product. Try to show that what is the solution you are providing to a problem in a line. Like a motor bike company can you use a tagline "Ride more, spend less" which clearly shows that the bike which they are offering will help the customers in saving more money and will give good mileage.

Show the path

- As soon as a potential customer gets interested in your product, give them a simple step to follow to reach to get more information or even the product itself. Add a step like interested people can call, text, email on this number or email. Or can visit your website.

There were key points to take care off while doing marketing to make it more effective. Moreover, if you build a good reputation in market, that reputation will again help you in terms of marketing. When you continuously improve your product, services and delivers most of the value as promised. It makes your customers to recommend your product to their knowns which is the most effective form of marketing than any other.

2. Sales

The most important and key segment of a business is sales because this is the major revenue generating process of any business. Sales can only be done, when you are able to convince your potential customers that whatever you are offering is the worth paying for as people don't like to be sold, but they like to buy. They don't want you to push them to buy anything.

"Sales is not about pushing the clients to purchase your product, it is about solving their problem"
-Rishabh Jain

Making a sale seems to be very tricky and complicated as every customer has different mind-set and different set of requirements, if your product or service doesn't fit their requirements, there is no way that they would like to pay you. So, you need to understand what your customer is actually looking for. Sales cannot be taught as it doesn't have any specific formulae which can be by heart. However, there are some points which you should remember before approaching a prospect.

Making a Transaction.

- In Ancient times, when there was no currency to purchase anything, what people used to do to buy things? They used to trade using the things they already have. If someone have something which other person want and the other person possess an item which they want. They do exchange things to do trade and complete a transaction. Making a transaction is always necessary to trade or to do business. Nowadays, we have money which we exchange for something we want and that's how trading works. A complete transaction is an essential part of a sale.

Importance of trust

- Trust is an another most important factor to complete a transaction. No one will pay you for anything which the person is not sure of that you will be able to deliver the value as per your promise. Same way, you will also not be able to provide value, until unless you are not sure that the prospect will be able to pay the price or not. That is why it is really important to have trust in between both the parties.

Match up

- Generally, when you have something to sell, then 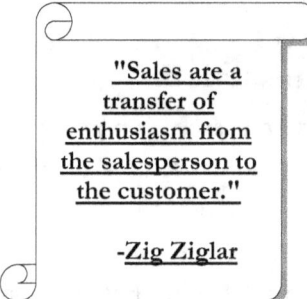 you will have a list of its features and benefits. Also, your potential customers will have a list of requirements. To make a sale, you just need to match the benefits of your products with the requirements of your customers. When both the lists will overlap, a sale is made. So you just need to check how you can create a common area between the requirements of prospect and benefits of your product.

"**Sales are a transfer of enthusiasm from the salesperson to the customer.**"

-**Zig Ziglar**

Right Pricing

- When someone wants to buy something, they try to get it on as less price as possible. A manufacturer or seller has the complete right to put any price on his/her product or service. They can ask for 100,000/- INR for a normal piece of stone and another second they can put the price as low as 1000/-INR for the same thing depending on the prospect. So the prices of any product can be variable but it should strictly worth the value being provided by your product and service (considering the price is above the making cost).

- Deciding and putting a price on your product and services will depend on certain factors. Those factors are: -

  ➢ The making cost of the product. Check how much did it cost you while building the product. Calculate the cost of making and put the price by adding a certain amount of margin of profit to it.

  ➢ The second thing will be the market price. Check that how much the other similar things are being sold for. To exist in a competitive market, you cannot put higher prices for the same product which is already available in the lesser price.

  ➢ Also consider that if you put the product on rent which can generate recurring income, how much it will be. Suppose, if you build a house, you can check that if you put it on rent how much a person will be willing to pay you. Calculate the rent and see what will be the best price to sell.

These factors will help you a lot in deciding the best price for your product.

Low Price is not a right track always

- There is a mentality of human mind-set "Lower the price, more the sales", which is actually not true in every case. Sometimes lowering the price of your product might destroy your business. An Iphone seems more attractive because of its high price as it is majorly dedicated to the status of people. They feel good about buying a smartphone which is of high value. It gives them a feeling of getting a good social status. So lowering the price does not work everywhere. You need to analyse your market first while working on the prices of your product.

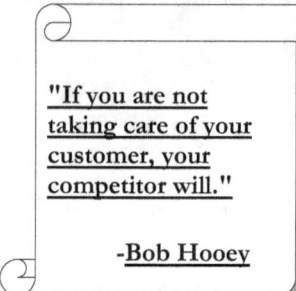

"If you are not taking care of your customer, your competitor will."

-Bob Hooey

Pricing doesn't have to depend on Expense

- More of the making cost and profit margin, pricing majorly depends on the value which you are providing to your customer. There is a possibility that a wrist watch which costs 1 lakh didn't take much making cost. However, as far as it is giving the value to the customer of social desire. Same way if you are providing a service to the company which is helping the company in raising crores every year, there is nothing wrong in charging few lakhs for the service even though there are not much efforts or resources are being used in providing the service. The company will still pay you a good amount as far as they are getting the benefits as per their expectations.

Educate and Sell

- Insurance companies do have many different policies with different prices and premiums. However, when they approach a prospect to sell a policy, they just not only tell about the basic benefits, they educate the customer about all the pros and cons about a particular policy. Which is an ideal way of dealing with a prospect. If you won't educate your prospect well about your services and product. There is a huge possibility that the customer won't be paying you. You could close the deal once by just convincing them but once they got to know that there is something which you didn't tell about to them, they will not continue purchasing from you. Tell them why your product or service is better than a competitor so that you can earn trust of your customer and build a long term relationship with them.

Offer Alternatives

- What if your offer is not meeting the requirements of your prospect and other competitors offering a good deal which your prospect is aware of? It means the prospect have an another best alternative. Now, what will be your next point of action. Before approaching any prospect, you need to research about your competitors. Check what are they offering and prepare for a better offer. Make a good combination of your offerings where you not only need to add but you can also remove some things which are not of best interests of your prospect. Offer the best package of your product or service which seems better than the another best alternative they have.

Right Negotiation

- Now comes the most important part, "Negotiation". If you are not good at it, there is a huge possibility that you won't be able to close a good deal. Negotiation or presenting an offer needs a good homework. As mentioned earlier, you need to research about the market and your competitors. Before approaching your prospect, create a good setup, check how you will be approaching a prospect. Is the deal going to happen in person, or on call or email? Prepare a proposal, structure it in the way the other party should feel interested in it. Check what are their requirements. Make a match of your offerings with their requirements. See where the other party might object.

Once you are ready to answer any possible queries and you are confident that you will be able to provide the better offer than the other competitor, you are ready to go.

Next part is, check who you will be negotiating with. Is the other person having the decision making power to finalize the deal or not? If you are approaching a young man or a kid, there is a high possibility that final decision will come from the parents or a guardian. Try to approach the final decision maker directly to deal with. Once you are done with all these, go ahead and present your offering with a good frame and in step by step manner. Answer every question being asked. Open to face the counter questions. Try to speak less and listen most of your customer. Give relevant rebuttals to show your offering as better than any competitor. Never push them to close the deal right away. Give your prospect time to think about it. There is a possibility that, even after giving your best. You are still not able to close it as the prospect is unable to make the final decision right away. In that case, be open to approach a new prospect. Sometimes, the prospects might not want to buy at all as of now. So, leave the deal on a good note. Tell them, they should feel free to contact you in future if needed for anymore further queries.

> "The most difficult thing in any negotiation, almost, is making sure that you strip it of the emotion and deal with the facts."
>
> -Howard Baker

There is a possibility that if a prospect is not able to buy from you right away may purchase from you in future. Keep yourself calm in the whole deal and be open to get a NO from your prospect.

Help from Mediators

- Sometimes, taking help from a mediator, attorney or an agent can be quite helpful while negotiating in a deal. As they are the experts of the particular field and will be able to help you in making the best decision. They act like a buffer where both the parties should be able to find a common ground between their requirements so that both the parties won't face any loss.

Right Approach

- It can be seen everywhere that if a salesperson tries to push the prospect to get a deal closed. There is a higher probability that the prospect won't make a deal. As people don't like to be pushed while making a financial decision. Whenever you approach a prospect, the prospect will always have an initial mentality that he or she might get tricked by the sales person to purchase something which is not of their best interests. So, if they feel that other party is trying to push them to make a sale, they will immediately back off from the conversation and try to just leave the deal. Make sure that whenever you are approaching a prospect frame your pitch accordingly that it should not seems to be pushy at all. Explain everything about your offering and how it can benefit the prospect in the best way. Be transparent about your offerings, people are attracted to honesty. Give them time to reach a final decision.

Offering for free

- You must have seen whenever you go to a good restaurant, hotel, showrooms or any big brand. They will always offer you something which seems like a goodwill like "would you like to have a cup of tea, coffee or a juice?" Because when you get something for free, it makes you feel that you should also give something in return. No, that is not only because they want to offer a goodwill. It is because they know how human psychology works. They know that if they offer something for free. There is a huge possibility that the prospect will surely buy something from them. They tie the prospect with the feeling of giving a favour in return by purchasing from them.

Transparency

- Nobody and nothing in this world is 100% perfect. You can be better than anything but cannot be perfect. Which means even your product and service will have some defaults. But that doesn't mean you try to hide those faults from your prospect, as they are also aware that there will always be some issues. Rather than waiting for them to find it. Tell them upfront while negotiating with them. Transparency is the key to a good business. It builds trust for you in prospect which they like to have if they are paying you.

Make it easy to decide

- When you want to buy something in the market. Let's say you want to buy some clothing, you go to the market and see tons of options to buy. Every shop has different sizes and design. And if the salesperson shows you 10 options to choose and they all look like good to you but you are only willing to buy 1-2. There is a huge possibility that you will get confused and will leave without buying anything. Here if the shopkeeper could have shown you 4 best options, it would have been very easy for you to pick 2 of them. That is how sales work, you do not have to present each and everything you have to offer Ask about the specific requirements of your prospect and accordingly filter out some of the best fits which you can show to your prospect and make it easy for them to make a decision so that they can pick the best one for them.

Still Got a 'NO'

- Even after your pitch was best, you have given your 100%. Still you get a 'NO' from your prospect. This could be because of some following reasons:
  - ➤ Suppose it seems to the prospect that your product is expensive. Here you need to explain that why your product or service is

worth paying the price. Explain them about the value being provided and why it is worth paying the amount.

➢ When the prospect thinks that the product won't work for them or it may work for others but not specifically for them as they have some exceptional set of requirements. Now you need to show them that how other people with same requirements are already taking the advantage of your product and it is working best for them. That is how referrals works the best as marketing. As it builds a trust in your new prospect when someone recommends your product.

➢ One more reason of a 'NO' could be when the prospect thinks that this is not the right time for them to purchase your product or service. Here education based selling will work. Where you need to make your prospect aware about the problem which you are solving with your product. They should be aware what is the problem they are facing exactly. And then explain them how your product can solve their problem in the best.

Offer Guarantee

• Even after you have applied every strategy mentioned earlier in this book. Still a prospect will always think of not taking a Risk of paying you for your product. What if your product will not provide the promised benefits? Their money will go into vain. After all, you are unknown to them. How they can be sure of paying you for anything you are offering?

This is one thing you can do, give them a money back guarantee offer. Which means give them a deadline as per your product where they can use your product for a specific time and try it. If the product doesn't work for them they can return the product and can get their complete money back. This is how you will be able to reduce the risk percentage for your prospect.

However, this can be a bit risky for you. As there is a possibility that even after the product was good for your customer. They have used it and still returned back to get their money back. Now you need to analyse that what will be the best time line you can put for the offer. You can put it as minimum as possible so that the product can be tested and if it looks good they should keep it. Also you can add certain terms and conditions for returning it. Which is like while returning the product should not be damaged or it should be in its original packaging. This will help in reducing the risk for you.

Approach Old Customers

- It could be a bit difficult for you to approach a new prospect every time to keep your business running. So the best way to make more sales is to approach your old customers and not only approaching new prospects. You can approach your old customers who have already used your product earlier. Present your updated product to let them buy again from you. It will be more beneficial than reaching new one's every time. Also, it will take less efforts and time to convert your inactive customers. That is how subscriptions work. TV service providers, ISPs Online streaming sites like Netflix, Hotstar etc. use this as their major strategy to keep business running. Keep a record of contact details of each and every customer so that you will be able to approach them again in future.

3. Value Delivery

A successful business always delivers whatever being promised to its customers. It delivers the complete value being promised for the price which is worth paying for it. Business which doesn't provides the promised value to its customers are called as to be scammed and won't exist in the market for the longer period of time. As its reputation will be destroyed, customers won't pay them again.

Let's have a look at some major points needs to be taken care off while providing the value to your customers.

Basic Steps of Value Delivery

- Firstly, let's have a look at how a value is being provided. There are certain steps need to be followed to provide the product.
  - ➢ It will start from gathering all the raw material.
  - ➢ Arranging and preparing them to get the final product.
  - ➢ The product will be packed and will go for final Inspection.
  - ➢ Than the product will be arranged to be shipped to whole sellers, retailers. After that the product will be displayed to the customers at the retailer's shop and will be there until a customer pay for it.
  - ➢ The product will also be directly delivered to the customers in online shopping.

This is how a value being provided to a customer which was being promised via marketing.

Different Forms of Value Delivery

- When you do a business, there are two ways of offering a value. Either you provide the direct value to the customers or you can provide it via mediators.

  Suppose you have a restaurant; there you will be providing value via entertaining your guests and offering them a good meal directly. Same way, nowadays we have the option of providing food via online food delivery facility. Where you can provide same value via adding an inter mediator as an online ordering platform. Moreover, product manufacturers work in the same way. They offer and deliver the

"**Future is about creating value. If we have tools to empower each other, more possibility is reality**"

-Jessica Jackley

value using whole-sellers, supermarkets and retailers as their mediators. They are unable to offer the product directly.

However, using an intermediator could go another way as well. As there is a possibility that intermediator may damage the product and won't deliver a perfect product which will ruin the reputation of the company. So you need to keep an eye on the mediators too.

Going an Extra Mile

- It is not only lies in providing the promised value to do a good business. To stand out the competition in the market. You need to deliver the value which is higher than the expectations. Suppose if you are providing a meal as per the customer's desire and providing a complimentary drink or a desert will make them feel delighted with your service. It will make them choose you whenever they want to dine out next time. Which will build a great reputation in front of your customers.

However, you need to remember that once you provide something which is above their expectations than you must be at least maintaining those expectations next time for every customer as reducing the offerings will damage your reputation.

Delivering Satisfaction

- As mentioned above, offering something above the expectations of your customers' needs consistency as no one wants to get their expectations violated. They want to get the same satisfaction again and again whenever they chose you.

  What will happen? When you go to your favourite restaurant and you find a change in taste in your favourite dish. It will be enough to destroy your meal experience and ultimately make you think twice before entering the same restaurant again. To keep you engaged, the restaurant will have to provide the same taste which you like the most. So, consistency and reliability are the most important factors needs to be taken care off if you are looking to go for a long run.

Best Quality

- To make any business successful, you need to provide the value with the best quality. If you compromise with the quality, there are very high chances that it will damage your repo. You need to very cautious about it. There are certain factors on which the quality of the product is being judged.

> ➢ Firstly, the performance of your product will be checked.
> ➢ What all features are being provided in a single product or service. More the features, better will be the quality.
> ➢ How much reliable your product is?
> ➢ How long it will work without any further investment?
> ➢ Is it easy to get it fixed, if anything goes wrong?
> ➢ Does it provide a good satisfaction to get a better social status?

These are certain factors on which the quality of a product and service is being judged. So, always keep them in mind before making an offer for the value you are providing.

Feel of Quality

- Sometimes, even if your product is good, there is a possibility that while using it, shows not up to the mark. In those cases, you need to analyse that how your product let the customer have a feeling of worth paying for it.

"**Quality in a service or product is not what you put into it. It is what the client or customer gets out of it.**"

For an example: A soap can only look good when it produces good amount of bubbles. A good soap with no bubbles will never give a satisfaction of using it. It is always mandatory to have a satisfaction of using the product.

Making Continuous Improvements

- While doing any business, you need to analyse some factors, which are as follows:

  - ➢ First thing to analyse is that how much you are earning in a specific period of time. Which can be per hour/day/week/month/year. This will help you in understanding what you are earning and how you can increase it.
  - ➢ Analyse how many units of your product are being made in a specific period of time. Try to minimize the time of production of a single unit. So that you can be able to create more and more units to sell.
  - ➢ Analyse how much time it is taking to satisfy any one customer. Suppose if you are running a restaurant or a salon, check how much time it is taking for you to serve one customer/guests completely. The more number of customers getting satisfied in a specific time, the better the business will be.

You need to take care of all these things to make improvements in your business.

Make Duplicates

- When you know that you are able to make your customers satisfied with the value you are providing and you need to make more and more customers satisfied. Here, is where making duplicate products or units has to be done. This is no need to design the same thing again and again. You just need to create a standard design at once which everybody is liking and make duplicate copies of it. This will help you in saving much more time. Also, you need to multiply the production by opening more manufacturing units to do mass production according to the demand in the market. Duplicating the product and multiplying the units will help you in satisfying more and more customers at the same time.

Scale it up

- Suppose if you have a dish which everybody likes however you are only able to serve 50 guests with the same dish in an hour and the demand is getting higher, if you won't be able to fulfil that, then it will diminish your guest's experience and will affect your reputation. So, now you will need to scale up your business and you need to duplication/multiplication at the same time. That is how all the food chains work. McD, KFC, Starbucks all are food business chains that have a huge demand in the market and because of scaling up their businesses, they are able to satisfy most of their customers.

Continuous Improvements

- Whenever you provide value and your customers are satisfied. Still after sometime the customers will get bored as according to the human psychology, humans start getting bored of using anything after sometime. They always need a change. So, there is always a scope of improvement in your product or service. However, when you are doing mass production, a small change will affect the whole production. Which means you need to analyse that how a small improvement can affect your customer's expectations. Make small improvements every day to ultimately improve the overall satisfaction of all your customers.

Create Barrier

- Create a barrier for your competitors to compete with you. Make improvements in your product every day, week, month, year. Live up to beyond the expectations of your customers. As apple is doing the same thing. Even though offering a mobile phone at much higher price. Its features and performance are always worth paying for it. Apple is always focused on improving its products which made it stand out of the huge competition. Improvements are must if you want to do a good business and want to stay for a longer period of time. Also, it creates a barrier for your competitors by giving them a new lever of task to overcome.

Use of Technology

- To run any business, there is always a need of equipment to get your product completed and ready to deliver. However, there are multiple type of equipment are available in the market to do the same task. The difference will be in their capability of doing the task. How soon and efficiently it can help you in building a product decides the performance of it. The higher the performance the more will be the price of equipment. Always, invest in good equipment to get more work done in less time with great efficiency and performance according to the demand.

Creating a System

- To run any business, there is always a series of steps need to be followed to get the final product or service and deliver it to customer. These set of steps are termed as system. A system is very important to run a business in an efficient manner. Any improvements need to be made in the product of service are easy to analyse when there is a system in your business. If you create a good system than only you will be able to automate the business which will lead to save a lot of time which might take very long time to deliver the value when there is no system. Anything without system will become messy and will lead to a lot of confusion. A business with no system will be not able to exist in the market for a long period of time.

4. Finance.

Here, is the most complicated segment of a business which seems like very confusing to understand as you see many numbers and mathematical formulas which creates fuss.

However, if you understand the basis terms of finance you will be able to calculate it easily. One thing you need to understand about finance is that you should know that how much money is going out and how much money is getting in and at the end is it sufficient amount you are keeping to run the business further or not. There are some basic terms of finance which we will discuss here.

Analyse Profit

- The first thing you need to check how much profit your business is making. Which means how much you are being left with after deducting all your expenses.

> Profit in business comes from repeat customers, customers that boast about your project or service, and that bring friends with them.
>
> -W. Edwards Deming

If you are not getting enough profit or you are just getting the amount of revenue which is only able to manage the expenses than that it means your business is in trouble. As whenever the expenses will increase the business will start getting in loss. Any business cannot last for long if it is not making enough profit to exist in the market. Always analyse that what you are being left with after doing all the expenses.

Check Profit Margin for better results.

- Keep a record of your profit margin, which means that to analyse that if you spend X amount of money in providing a value to your customer and you earn Y amount of money than Y should be greater than X. And to get it calculated in terms of percentage there is a basic formula for that.

(Earning-Expenditure/Earning)*100=Profit Margin%

This is the basic formula which you can use to calculate your profit margin so that you will be able to understand what is the percentage of profit you are earning in a specific period of time or on a specific unit you are selling.

Low or High Profit Margin

- Another thing you need to check is that how much profit margin you are keeping, which means you need to check if you are not charging a lot money for providing small value as in that case, you will not be able to make sales because no one wants to pay more in exchange of small value which doesn't seem to be worth. For example: if you are offering a value to your customer which can bring 1 Million for him, charging 999,999 for your product or service will never make your customer to pay you for it.

So charge maximum amount of profit margin until it is justified to the value you are providing so that you will make good sales with enough profit margin.

There is another perspective comes when we speak about profit margin when you have a good competition in the market, it becomes very important to reduce your prices however you still need to check that you should charge at least the amount which should give you profit which is again important for business to run for a long time.

Satisfaction of Earning

- Doing a business doesn't mean that you always have to make millions or billions to keep your business running. It doesn't have to be a great big industry always. If you are generating enough revenue to pay your bills for everything and you are getting enough time to do whatever you want. Than you are already in the right pace to go forward.

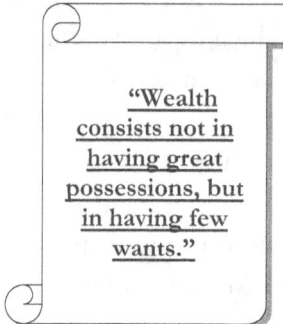

"Wealth consists not in having great possessions, but in having few wants."

One day, I approached my father and asked him why he doesn't scale up his business by hiring new workers and manager to manage this particular factory and open a new one. This is how you can focus on building a new factory so that you can generate more revenue. You can maximize the business and you will be able to earn much more.

He told me something which left me mum for a point of time. He said when I do all this it will take a lot of time and efforts and at last what I will get? Some more money but I don't need that I am satisfied with what I am getting. As now I am already able to pay all of your and other family member's expenses and still get time to spend with you all. I am able to satisfy mine and all your needs.

So the point is that if your business is generating sufficient revenue than there is no need to go above if you are satisfied. You just need to calculate how much money is needed to keep the business running and keep yourself satisfied. Analyse how much you need every month to keep your business running and set a target for yourself. Which is sufficient. If you are getting enough revenue than you are on right pace.

Working for High Valuation

- Every company or business has some valuation in total, which shows how promising a business is. When you have good profit margins, good revenue, good bank balance and ultimately you have enough to run the business for a long term, high the value will be of your company. A high valuation is always helpful when you are seeking for investors as high the valuation more will be the trust the investors will have in your company and it will feel worth investing their money. Also, the high valuation will also increase the share price of your company when it goes public.

Calculating Cash Flow

- To check the performance of your company, the simple sorted way is to check the cash flow statement. Now how does this works?

  A cash flow statement is where you can check how much cash is coming in via sales and investing and how much cash is going out in Marketing, Manufacturing, Equipment, Maintenance and paying dividends to shareholders. So you need to subtract cash going out from cash coming in and check if you are getting a good high value or not. It this calculation results in zero that means there is something wrong going on. Check where you are spending extra or your business is not making enough money to keep the business running. This will also help you in analysing how much capital you need from your investors. The more amount you are getting after subtracting the more beneficial it is as it will show how much money you are keeping after doing all the expenses.

Don't rely only on Cash Flow

- Calculating cash flow for your business and relying on it can be a loss case as well. Let's say if someone is purchasing a product to sell from a whole seller on credit which means the person doesn't have to pay right away to whole seller. Now the person or retailer will have some time to pay for the product and will be able to sell the product to consumers on cash. Which means the cash flow statement will look good as of now but when the time comes up to pay the whole seller than the real picture will show the profit earner. Obviously, the major purpose of a business is getting the maximum profit but cash flow calculation is not enough to judge the profit. Than you need to also calculate the profit earned which can be calculated in Income statement. Where you will check what is the revenue being generated and then subtract the expenses including the (cost of goods sold, expenses, taxes). Than you will get the real profit earned on one good. And that will help you in analysing that where you should cut the extra expenses to increase the profit. Otherwise, only cash flow calculation may lead to run out business as you won't be able to see what is the actual profit you are earning.

Balance Sheet

A balance sheet is a clear picture of your overall net worth, which gives you an idea that where your business stands.

A balance sheet calculates the value for your company for a specific day. It can be calculated via simple formula, where you need to Subtract your liabilities from your assets to see the result as what you are left with.

Assets-Liabilities= Your Equity

Let's take an example, suppose you borrow 1 lakh rupees from a bank and you already have assets of the value 200000. Now your balance sheet will be

$$300000-100000=200000$$

Now, what does it mean. It means that you have got 1 lakh of cash added as a liability to your company as you have taken a debt. And it will also get added to your asset column too. When you will start paying back to bank the digits will change. Suppose you pay 50000 to the bank. Now it will be

$$300000-50000=250000$$

Which can also be written as 300000=250000+50000. This is how you can check your company's net worth using the balance sheet. Whichever formula you take from above, both the sides should be equal to get the correct answer and if they are not equal that means you have made some error.

These calculations are not only to get a fancy financial excel sheets, these are important when you need to make financial decisions. They will always help you in analysing that which part of your business is working fine and which one needs to be fixed.

Keep analysing such data on timely basis to keep your business's financial health good. The best way to analyse is by comparing the financial ratios, check the profit ratios using profit margin to see how much your company is making in specific amount of time and if it is not enough you are making that means you need to work on your profit margin.

Now that we have gone through different segments of business, you must have got a clear and fair idea, how a business works and how can you start a business. What are all things which you need to take care off while doing a business? Although, this is not all about it, a book can always give you a theoretical knowledge however, that is not enough to do business. A practical knowledge is well needed which can only be gained when you actually do it.

Note: If you want to get more deep knowledge about business and finances, "The Personal MBA" by Josh Kaufman is highly recommended.

Notes:

Part-3

Working in the best way.

Now that you got to know that how does a business work and how can you start a business, let's learn that how our brains work and What are the best ways of working in a Business.

1.

<u>How does our Brain Works?</u>

Now as we have gone through how a business works now we need to learn how can we work with others and what are the best ways to do a business. Making any decision is really important to consider. We will be going to learn how we can make good decisions in terms of doing business.

In Ancient times, it was an era where everyone needs to take care of food, shelter and clothing. There were no facilities like we have today and moreover we do not have certain life threatening challenges that our ancestors used to have.

A hundred thousand years ago, the challenges were so different in our ancestor's life that they were not sure about how they will survive in next day of their life. Challenges like getting food every day from plants or sea food. Catching and hunting an animal every day. Safety was also used to be a major concern as they used to live in forests where they have to secure themselves from certain wild animals. However, the era has been changed now. Today, you do not have to worry about that, you have got food, shelter and clothing sorted by our ancestors. Now you have certain more challenges in your life. You have to go to office, complete certain tasks, get your job done on time. But our bodies are same. Now we do have more challenges with our brains. Which creates new diseases like obesity, stress, heart attacks and much more.

So the point is that you do not have to be so hard on yourself as all of our brains and bodies are same as that off our ancestors. Don't take too much stress of anything, life is one and you need to decide how would you like to live it. Either you can live it in stress creating so much trouble to your health or you can be live it happily by continuously working in a certain direction without much stress.

Requirements of Working Efficiently

All our bodies have certain requirements which are needed to be fulfilled in order to work in a certain way. You cannot work well for a long time if you do not give your body what it actually needs. As a Vehicle needs fuel to run, you also need certain fuel to run your body and brain efficiently.

> Obviously, the highest type of efficiency is that which can utilize existing material to the best advantage.
> -Jawaharlal Nehru

1. The first requirement is food. You need to have good quality food with balancing your diet to be healthy. You need to balance your diet with healthy and tasty food. If you will always

have healthy food with no good taste than after sometime you will get bored of it and won't feel good. So certain cravings need to be fulfilled to be stress free and happy. Although this should be done vice-versa.

2. Second requirement is exercise. A certain physical body exercise is always needed in order to keep yourself active and working. Otherwise, it will not let you work for a longer period of time.
3. Third requirement is sleep; you should have at least 6 hours of sleep everyday so that your body gets recharge to work more. Don't take it lightly as it can be a serious issue to your health in long term.
4. Another last but not the least thing is sun light. You should get enough sunlight in order to get your body absorb some light and heat energy.

These are certain major requirements needs to be fulfilled in order to work efficiently.

Things Under Control

Your body has certain setup points where if any point is violated than something needs to be done to take the situation back to that certain set point in order to get things under control. For example, if you are in a normal temperature than there is nothing extra needed to be done but suddenly you start feeling cold as the temperature of environment goes down than you need to wear more clothes to get yourself back to the normal situation of not feeling cold.

Similarly, in a business you always have a certain amount of revenue needs to be generated on a timely basis in order to keep the business running, if your business is not generating the revenue than it means something needs to be fixed in order to get things under control.

Same way if you are getting more and more complaints in your customer service department than usual, check what is going wrong in order to clear the complaints.

Things and situations are meant to be in control according to the range or set points which are being setup by you in your business.

Now sometimes, you feel that even the situation is up to the mark of set point and you feel still there is some issue or situation is under control than it means you need to make changes to the set point or range.

The point is that if you are getting a feeling that something is not right than changes needs to be done either in the situation or set up points and ranges.

Satisfaction of life

There are always two types of people, one who are happy with their routine life where they have a secured job or business which is giving them enough money to spend their life happily. They are able to pay their bills on time and they are able to

> No amount of money can replace the kind of happiness and satisfaction I derive out of writing.
> -Sreenivasan

complete their desires in whatever they are earning. In such cases, these people don't bother to make any changes in their life. They are not making themselves bother about trying something else which might work better. So their energy is conserved. And ultimately they are satisfied with their 9-5 jobs and don't even want to get out of the rat race.

However, the second category of people are the ones who are not satisfied with their life, they have a sense of feeling that they are not making enough to fulfil their desires. People like me are always trying to seek something which can make their desires to be fulfilled however whenever they achieve something they get another point of dissatisfaction and a new desire to work on. This point of dissatisfaction made me write this book as I don't want to keep whatever knowledge I have to myself. And hence they do not have much energy conserved in their life.

So now it's up to you, check which category you are falling in and what you should do to make yourself get back in to a certain point where you will feel that your desires are being fulfilled.

Behavioural Change

Suppose if you have a habit or behaviour which you want to change in order to be more productive in your life. Let's say you want to quit a habit of drinking soda or soft drinks. Now you feel it's not easy for you to quit as you are unable to resist your cravings.

The easiest way to help you out is that stop buying them, keep yourself away from the scope of seeing it on your table, fridge or anywhere. Stop being with people who do have it regularly. This way you will get a help in resisting yourself of having them.

It is useful because according to our nature, everyone is lazy. Nobody wants to put extra efforts of doing anything. When you will keep yourself away from things than it will become difficult for you to get them and it will also help you in getting a high will power of resisting your cravings.

Same way, changing your environment can help you in changing your habits. If you want to start going to Gym, make your environment surroundings like that. Be with Gym freaks, get yourself some gym friendly equipment. Prepare your things a night before you want to go to the gym. Like keep your gym bag and clothes ready so that as soon as you get up you will have easy access to take them and leave.

Situations where you are unable to get things under control

There is a possibility when you get a feeling that there is something wrong in your job and you are not getting complete satisfaction which you are seeking for. However, you are also not able to understand the reason of this dissatisfaction. That is where you try something new by joining a new company where you do the same work for different people. Now again you are still not able to get on the right path. There are two things can be done, either you force yourself to be in the same job by convincing yourself that everything is fine or you continue to try something until you get the right thing.

Here, both things can be done. Now you need to figure out that is it worth of taking any one of the actions. Check that is it really hard for you to stay in the same job. If the answer is yes than, please go ahead and look for something new. But if you feel that yes it is not that much you need to bother about than you can stay and convince yourself.

Fight between Thoughts

Has this ever happened with you where you have some task to complete however you don't want to do it right now because it doesn't feel to be that important. You decide to do it after some time after taking a nap or so. But still your mind is thinking that you should do it or not. You are not feeling peace in not doing it neither

> We are what our thoughts have made us; so take care about what you think. Words are secondary. Thoughts live; they travel far.
>
> -Swami Vivekanada

you want to do it. This is where when you have fight between your thoughts. This is called procrastination which is normal with everyone. As everyone has n number of tasks to do and Some of them needs to be done on priority however others are not. And you are unable to decide which one you should do first. This is where your set up point is disturbed and you are struggling to get it back to normal. Because your thoughts are fighting in your inner self.

Another example in terms of business which we can use here to understand it better is when you allocate a responsibility to one of your employee and others feel bad about it, where another conflicts happen as all of them have different satisfaction setups and ranges. Again fight happens.

The solution to such fights is to change the setup points. In case of where you are unable to decide which task to do first, the solution is organize. Organize your task time and rest/lavish time, create a time table for yourself without ignoring lavish time.

In case of employee fights, change the setup points of employees by giving them separate responsibilities by dividing a big responsibility into parts.

Learning through Patterns

What happens when you get your hands on a burning candle? Obviously, you pull your hands out. As you already know it will burn you and you will feel pain. Now did it take time for you to learn that fire is bad. No, while you were in your child age, automatically you got that it is harmful and dangerous to touch fire. That is how there are much more scenarios which you learn automatically by patterns. That is why there are many things which can only be learned by experiences.

When any of your things get lost, what is the first thing you do to search it. You think where all have you been and where possibly you could have left it. That is again pattern matching. It can be very useful in terms of work life as well. An experienced person will always work better than a person with no experience as the experienced person have already faced some things which a fresher is not aware off. An experienced person will be able to immediately solve an issue which might be difficult for a fresher and that is because of learning through patterns.

Suppose if a company wants to test something, they want to take advice from the employees. They give a situation to everyone and wants to know how this will work. In such scenarios, an experienced person will be the better person to tell the result or solution as the person might have gone through such scenarios earlier as well.

Mental Stimulation and Imagination

Our brains work maximum times on Imagination. Whenever you get a situation or a question, your mind starts working on it and gives you results after going through the patterns which are already stored. Suppose if you plan to travel to a cool place, your mind will give you some points to consider before making any arrangements. Like you have to get some warm clothes,

> The world of reality has its limits; the world of imagination is boundless.
>
> -Jean-Jacques Rousseau

you need to buy the tickets to travel etc. This has been done by your mind without making you do some action. Now this helps in business too, if you have a question for any future changes, you will start getting the answers from your brain before taking any action on it. However, those answers might not be correct every time.

Have you ever received any message which made you angry as your mind has given you a thought that the tone which was used in the message was wrong? Now after meeting that person you come to know that it was not the tone which you have imagined while you got the message. This means that your brain has misinterpreted that message and you have to reinterpret to get the best results. So never go with the first result which you get from your brain without making sure about it. This can become a big loss in your business too.

Sometimes, when you do not have the complete information about the situation than whatever results your brain gives can be right too. Suppose if you listen something about someone and make up a bad image about that person according to the things which have been told to you. Now after listening to the victim again you correct your brain by creating the right picture. Now it doesn't mean that the picture you have got earlier was a mistake of your brain. It is just that the earlier picture was being created only using the information which you had. So as mentioned earlier you need to have a look on both the sides of a coin.

Being Motivated and Working for Status

Motivation may be the most popular word. But what does it mean actually? When you want to achieve something, you think that what you need to do to achieve it. Now your plan of action has a lot of risk. Now it becomes difficult for you to decide whether you should do it or not. Here is when the motivation comes into picture which is an emotional state of your brain. If you are well motivated to take the action in order to achieve your goal, you overcome that risk and take the action. However, if you are too afraid of taking the risk to achieve your goal than you becomes demotivated. This means there is a conflict in your brain. Now your sense of achieving your goal should be strong enough to overcome the risk of losing something. That is when you can say that you are motivated to take the action in order to achieve your goal.

Let's understand this by taking an example, suppose if you want to start your own business and you are working in a high paying job. You need to lose the job in order to do business which makes you feel afraid to taking that risk. Now you should be motivated enough to overcome that fear of losing the job in order to take action and achieve your desire. That is how motivation works.

You must have heard that why to put money in expensive or luxurious things when you can get your needs fulfil by purchasing economic products. If you require a mobile phone than you can get an affordable mobile phone, why to put a good amount in buying an apple I phone.

Why people buy luxurious cars, watches, phones etc.? When they can get all these needs fulfilled by purchasing economical products.

Because it is not a matter of fulfilling a need but to have a good social status. There are many things which are being opted to have a good social status. A luxury watch will give you the same time which an affordable watch can give. But it will highly affect your social status.

A person who gets a gold medal in Olympic Game, that gold medal alone is not at all worth of the years of practice he/she has done. But that gold medal gives the best social status which is being recognized worldwide as the sign of victory and being the best. Sometimes it doesn't relate to the value of the material or the skill but the social status attached with that thing.

The conclusion is that in this Modern Era, people are not behind to fulfil basic needs as they are already been taken care off. Most of us are running behind to achieve a good social status. Sometimes this run costs a lot to a person who doesn't calculate the risk is being taken by him/her and at the end they get nothing. No matter how much you practice and how much efforts you give to achieve what you want, at the end there are limited positions to achieve and there is a huge competition to get those limited positions.

Now running behind social status becomes risky because you cannot predict whether giving all your time and efforts will pay you back or not. So choose wisely the way to your destiny.

Fear is stronger than belief

Whenever you want to try something new, there are always two thoughts around it.

First is when you think about the results being good for you which keep you motivated. However, as per the human tendency there is always a fear of losing something if you try it. And sometimes this fear becomes stronger than the belief of getting good results.

When you plan to start a new business, you risk money, efforts and the security of a job if you are working somewhere. And that fear of losing these things is somewhere higher than building own business.

There are lot of people who wants to have their own business and comparatively very few people goes ahead. Why so, that is because of the fear of losing the things which they have as of now. To overcome this situation, you just need to reinterpret in your mind that the risking all these things is not a big deal in front of the dream of achieving your goals.

These fears block you from trying something good and keep you running in the same rat race. If you have good action plan than go for it.

Don't let fear stop your way to your destiny.

Decision Making Power

Imagine you are at a higher position in an organization and you have a decision making power. You have a situation where you need to make some big decisions for the betterment of the organization however your decision might affect a lot of people working in the company.

Here in this situation, many people take the decision without even thinking about the people who all are working for them.

This demotivates them a lot. Now, it is not being done intentionally because the decision maker is not able to think about a lot people at the same time as there is a limitation to a human brain that our brains are not able to cater more than 150 people together. People more than 150 start acting like an object to our brains. This makes it difficult for the decision maker to think about all those together.

There are two ways to get a resolution in such situations. If the decision maker will think in this way that if this decision will come in front of their grandchildren in future, what they will think about you? This will make the people think twice before making any decision and they will also think that how their decision will affect all those workers out there.

There is one more way to think in a different way. If a decision maker thinks that what will happen if their decision will become a news headline for tomorrow's newspaper than what will happen? This again will make the decision maker think twice before making any decision. These two scenarios help multiple people in making the right decision.

Notes:

2.

Working as an Individual or with others.

Now that you have seen that how our brains work, let me tell you how do we work alone and how do we work with others.

It may sound like not a very important thing to know however it will give you a clear picture of how you can make your working effective and efficient.

Procrastination

The most common topic or term comes up in our mind while we think about being productive is "Procrastination".
This is the biggest and most common problem of most of the individuals.

Now in procrastination, it is of two types:

1. Where you know that you need to do something and you are just keep on scheduling it for future without actually taking an action on it.
2. The second scenario is where when you just only think about doing something where you are not even sure about doing it. Let's say you want to quit a bad habit but you are not even sure of it that when you should start taking action on it.

These two scenarios are the biggest issues while we talk about the productivity of an individual. Most people are aware that they are doing procrastination; still they are not able to overcome that issue.

This can only be done when you start managing and organizing your day to day task. Create a to-do List every day for your daily task.

The tasks should be in the order of priority. Keep the most important and most boring task to be done at the first time you start doing anything. And the order should go further; this will really help you in completing your task and minimize the procrastination. You will have a fair idea about what are all tasks you need to do today or tomorrow.

Moreover, it is not always necessary to be too harsh on yourself. Sometimes taking a lavish time for you is also very important.

So organize your work and make right decision so that you can be productive for the maximum of your time.

Multitasking

Here is the most hyped technique of completing your daily task, which seems to be very effective. It seems very smart to do multitasking when it comes to being productive. But at the same time, when anyone try to do something together, the efficiency of the task get affected. Our brains are not built to do multitasking. When anyone try to do multitasking, it actually seems that you are putting your efforts to do multiple task together but you are actually shifting your attention to do them.

Let's understand this by taking an example. Suppose I am driving and taking a call. It seems that I am doing multitasking but I am just shifting my mind from one task to another very quickly. Try to think about it once for yourself too. You will realize that your brain is not able to think about two tasks together. Your brain is just shifting quickly from one task to another. So it's a myth that a one can do multitasking. And if you try to do it that means your efficiency will be affected, sometimes badly.

> The secret to multitasking is that it isn't actually multitasking. It's just extreme focus and organization.
> -Joss Whedon

So always, schedule your task. Make a to-do list every day to complete your work timely and efficiently. If you will try to do multitasking, you will waste your energy and end up getting nothing. The better is you plan everything, divide your minor and major tasks, plan them and execute.

You can also delete the tasks from your list which aren't important or if anything is unnecessary. This will reduce your list and make it more confined.

Sometimes, there are some of your tasks which you can assign to someone else as well, which will help you a lot in saving your time.

You can also keep some tasks aside as of now, as there are some tasks which are not necessarily to be completed now or are not urgent.

Make a confined and crisp to do list according to the priorities of your tasks and work on that.

Setting Right Goals

Sometimes, the major issue of being frustrated and confused in life is that we don't set up right goals in our life.

> "Setting goals is the first step in turning the invisible into the visible."
> -Tony Robbins

The goals which we set up in our life should be the right ones. That means if you want to achieve something, than you should have a proper scenario of achieving it. Let say if someone want to win a gold medal in Olympics. Than just setting up goal like this will never let you work in direction of achieving it. Because to win a gold medal in Olympics, you need to check that in which sports or game you want to win and what is the best sport for you. How much time you will take to master it? This things needs to be cleared beforehand.

Without all this information, you won't be able to work at all. Set your goals with specific time range. Give yourself a range of deadline that until this age or until this time you should achieve a particular thing.

Apart from this, many people have goals of achieving success in their life where they don't even know that at what point they will consider that they have achieved it. As success has different meaning for each and every person. So achieving success or happiness is not a goal, it's just an emotion which you will get after achieving what you wanted to.

The goals which you are setting up should be positive. And never get demotivated if you don't achieve something in given point of time. Suppose if you set up a goal of not getting fat, there is a possibility that even after making all the efforts you don't achieve it in specific time. Keep going until you achieve the desired results. Because you never know how much time it may take. Instead you can set up a goal of doing exercise daily and controlling your calories on daily basis. This will keep you fit and motivated.

Interests and Notice

A couple of months back, I have started gaining interest in SUV Cars which gradually increased day by day. I have started liking particularly 2 models and suddenly I have seen that there are a lot of those 2 models are there running on the way which I have never noticed earlier. It seemed to me like suddenly many people have started buying those cars. This is not actually correct. The cars were already there, it is just that I was noticing them earlier. This happens when our brain starts gaining interest in particular things.

You can also try that, pick anything which makes you feel good and you want to acquire that thing as soon as possible. You will realize that you have started noticing that particular thing more often around you. And it's not like that thing has appeared suddenly around. It was already there but your brain was not noticing it. This is the power of your brain.

Whenever you have a goal to achieve, start taking interest in that and you will see the things you need to achieve that goal will start appearing around you. The same thing happens in being motivated as well. If you will look at your problems, your brain will start noticing more problems for you and when you will take interest and seek for resolution, you will start getting ideas for a solution.

So now it's up to your thoughts and interests. Use your brain for yourself in an effective way. You need to start seeking for solutions, rather than taking interest in problems to get motivated and work for your Goal.

Making Commitments

Making Commitments or Decisions is the most typical thing of our life. Many of us become so confused in our life and make it difficult to take a decision. This affects a lot. As when we are not on a conclusion than we won't be able to focus on anything in our life.

When any decision is made, we close all the other possibilities which makes it easier for us to focus on the thing which we want to do finally. Sometimes we are unable to decide which thing or action will work best for us, as there are many options around us to pick and it makes us confused. It seems to be no solution to it.

> **Individual commitment to a group effort - that is what makes a team work, a company work, a society work, a civilization work.**
>
> **-Vince Lombardi**

This happens because we never have complete information for any possibility, as we can never predict future. Than what is the solution?

In such cases, you just need to have maximum 70% of information for any possibility and rest your guts will work. You can also think about it this way, check every possibility and see which possibility or actions will work best for you.

Which one will give you the best feeling? You just need to figure out the one which will have the more possibility to work in your favour.

It is very important for everyone to get this situation resolved as soon as they get it. Because this confusion becomes so high and will let you go nowhere in your life.

Open your mind, think about it, consult it and take a good decision.

Working Step by Step

Whenever you have a goal, you start thinking about all the actions you need to take in order to achieve it. Which ultimately puts you in confusion that which step you need to take first to reach the destination. And you just keep roaming around here and there.

The best way to work on it is that you take your goal as your new project and break it into steps. Think of the very first step you need to take in order to climb the first ladder. Don't focus on all the actions altogether. Write down all the steps and segregate the most important steps needs to be taken. Make an order for those actions. Then start working on them one by one. Until you are done with your first step, don't think about second one. This way you won't get confused. Being consistent will give you results which will keep you motivated.

There is one better way to work on it. When you have multiple thoughts, there are chances that it won't let you start working step by step as it will keep roaming around your head. Start writing your thoughts or start speaking about it with the person you are comfortable with. This will give you a much better clear picture of your thoughts. You will be able to identify and prioritize your actions. As when you start clearing out your mind by expressing your thoughts, you get more space to think about it further.

Fear caused by Thoughts

Each and every one of us has a fear of losing. Whenever we think of starting a business or doing something which is not 100% predictable creates fear inside us which resist us to work on that.

When anyone wants to start any business, they think that they would need to quit their job, need to put some amount as investment and need to have some capital to keep it running for some time until it starts working in your favour. It creates thought of losing many things; it will let you think that what will happen if the business doesn't work. You will have a huge mortgage to pay, you might go bankrupt, everyone will see you like a culprit and your life will become hell. These thoughts let you keep behind and you don't move forward.

This is all because your brain is overthinking and overreacting for the situation. Just ask yourself, even though if your plan doesn't work, how max it can affect you? Don't let yourself get demotivated because of the negative predictions you are getting. The prediction of bad results should not take over the joy of getting the good results. As this is not something which is life threatening. If you have a good plan and you know what all steps should be taken in order to get the best results and you are sure that you have at least 50% of the information you need in order to achieve your goal than go for it.

Never let your fear stop you to work on achieving your Goal.

Overconfidence

Confidence, the word everyone has exaggerated a lot in their life. Since childhood we are listening about it. If anyone wants to achieve anything, confidence is something which has to be must. Without confidence, there is nothing we can achieve. However, as we all know anything which is above the limit is harmful for us. If we are not sure about the actions which we are taking or planning to take then there is no point of moving forward. All of your doubts need to be cleared before taking an action. Until you have faith in yourself, you won't be able to give your 100% in order to achieve your goal. Your doubts will hold your hands to take all the important steps.

> **Never be afraid to fail. Failure is only a stepping stone to improvement. Never be overconfident because that will block your improvement.**
> **-Tatchakorn Yeerum**

However, there is another side of it too. When this confidence becomes over confidence with anyone, it starts destroying the people. Somebody with overconfidence starts losing the interest in taking care of the actions. Many times it turns out to be a huge loss to people.

Anyone gains confidence when they look after each and everything, consider all the consequences and then become ready to take further steps. However, when a person starts gaining overconfidence, it makes him/her careless and the person doesn't care to consider all the parameters before taking any action. This affects a lot in long term.

To avoid such issues, we need to be confident but not overconfident. You should be able to realize that when you are entering in the stage of being overconfident. When you start ignoring every advice being offered and start thinking that you are the only person who knows best.

It is not only being confident about yourself, it is about your faith in yourself and other things too. When faith becomes blind faith, it creates chaos. When somebody stops reasoning than the blind faith starts and people get destroyed.

Have faith after making sure about all the things, considering all the things around it. Never be overconfident about anything in your life.

Time and Energy

As we all know, we have very limited time. There are only 24 hours in a day. And you have to manage all the things. Sometimes it becomes quite difficult to manage all the chores in those 24 hours and you have to sacrifice your sleep in order to get all the things completed.

Our body doesn't have unlimited energy, everybody needs rest in order to get recharged again. Each of us has their own capability of working in a day. Some of us need 8 hours of sleep every day depending upon the time schedule. People who are working in night shifts doesn't really get complete sleep as the sleep in night is must for a human body as that is when you get complete relax. When you start working, your energy starts getting drained. And after couple of hours you will feel completely exhausted and you would require a nap to get recharged.

So now you need to manage, your energy in order to be fully productive. Divide your day according to your energy levels. You know when you are fully charged and able to do as many tasks as possible in specific time. When you are energetic, you are able to do as much as you can with maximum speed.

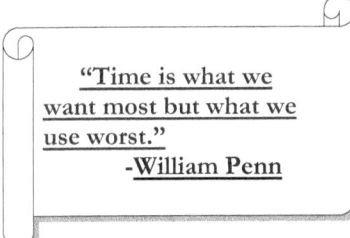

"Time is what we want most but what we use worst."
-William Penn

Keep your most important and time consuming tasks for the time when you are full charged and make an order of priority of all the tasks according to your energy levels drain by the day. And when you fell exhausted in the middle of the day. It's better to take a short break. You can go for some entertainment or relaxation in order to get charged again.

Apart from this, you can also check your maximum tendency to work in a specific time. To check this, you need to push yourself as much as you can while working without taking any specific break from work. Try to push as much as you can and you will see that this is your maximum tendency to work for anything.

It will help you in organizing many things. Suppose if you get a big project to work on with a certain deadline to complete it. Now if you don't know that what is your maximum tendency and what is the time where you can be maximum productive. There are high chances that you won't be able to complete your project on time. So you need to have an idea about yourself in order to make the most efficient working schedule.

Analyse your capability and give your best.

Attractive Ideas and Reality

Each and every one of us has some wants in our lives. Everybody has different wishes. Some wants to achieve high paying job, some wants to get fame, some wants to have peace in their life etc.

> **A dream doesn't become reality through magic; it takes sweat, determination and hard work.**
> **-Colin Powel**

However, not everyone is ready to pay in return. If someone wants to get raise or want to get promotion as it seems to be attractive but in reality they will also get a bigger responsibility to handle, they will get more work to do, which nobody wants to face. So our expectations of getting our dreams fulfilled seem to be attractive but in reality we are ready to accept the challenges which we need to face.

Anybody want to build high paying business seem to be really attractive however the person need to make same amount of efforts and need to take same amount of Risk in order to achieve the goal. When people get to know about reality they get demotivated.

Nobody likes to make the efforts which their dream actually requires. Now it doesn't mean that one should not have wants and dreams. However before setting expectations for yourself, you should have a good knowledge of the reality and you should be ready to accept it.

Now how would you know about the exact reality? You should ask the person already having the things which you are trying to achieve. The person will be the best to help you with the efforts need to make in order to achieve the goal. After consulting such people you will get a clear picture of reality and then you should think that whether you are ready to accept it or not.

Loss of Interest

When I was in 10th Standard, I have dreamed of getting a new scooter for myself to travel. I was so excited to get it and on my 18th Birthday my dad has gifted me the one. I have gone delightful as it was the thing which I wanted to have since couple of years. And after using it for couple of days and months, I have started losing interest in that. It was quite surprising that the thing which I wanted to get since couple of years, after getting it, I have started losing interest in that in couple of days.

The same thing happens with kids. You can notice this, whenever you get a new toy for a baby. At first they will play with it a lot but gradually they start losing interest in that and look for something new. This is a human nature, whenever we dreamed of achieving something in our life, it do makes us happy a lot when we achieves it but after sometimes we starts losing interest in that achievement and look for a new goal or thing we want to get. There is no definition or end point of success in one's life.

If somebody wants to be a millionaire, they work for it very hard and when they achieve a certain amount; they start feeling that it is not enough. There is specific thing in this world which can make you happy until your last breathe.

You need to think about it that whatever you are working for, till how much time it will be able to keep you satisfied. Is it really worth of putting those efforts? This question is not to demotivate you, but it is to showcase the reality. However, never lose yourself or your family in order to achieve something which is not worth.

It is not always money or materialistic thing which will keep you happy. It's your experiences in your life. The time you spend with your family and friends. The time you spend alone in peace. Look after all these things to judge whether your efforts worth the things you are trying to achieve or not.

Comparison and Control

The biggest reason of frustration in everyone's life is that they compare. Everybody is trying to compare themselves with others. If anyone achieves their goal in their life, we start feeling bad about it as if it's affecting them which is not at all true.

If your neighbour is buying a new car, you will never look at the efforts they could have made to but it but you will surely compare. This will make you feel bad and possibly will become a reason of huge frustration.

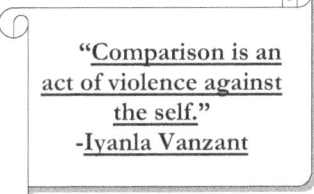

"Comparison is an act of violence against the self."
-Iyanla Vanzant

This is an unnecessary frustration which you are keeping with yourself and that can be released if you don't compare. Everyone has their own life, priorities, goals and requirements. Everybody is facing their own situations in life. There is no point of comparing. So it is better to feel good about it and appreciate them. It will help you in focusing on your goals and you will be much more productive in your life.

Apart from this there is one more thing which is again a big cause of frustration which is that we try to control all of the things in our life. Again this is not possible for anyone to control everything.

When you start any business or look for a new better job profile. If you are giving 100% of your efforts to it, still there is a possibility that you won't get desired results which you cannot control. Nobody knows what is going to happen in future. So it is better to work on the things which you can control and don't worry about the things which are out of control for everyone.

Don't let these things to be a best recipe of your Frustration.

Continuous Learning

Whenever, you are at a level and your desires are still pending. You need to make a research on yourself that what is the thing in you which needs to be improved. And it is not only needed when you are desires are not fulfilled. There is always a scope of learning for everyone. So as a habit everyone should make a small investment to do research and development on themselves. If we won't improve than our conditions won't too.

When I have started working as an agent, I was getting a good pay which was even satisfactory for me too. However, when the life goes on, our needs and wants changes by it. It started giving me a feeling that it is not enough for me and I need to get on a higher position. For that obviously I have started improving my skills in order to get on a higher position. Moreover, when I have started reading books, I realized that there is a whole a lot I need to learn and it won't stop until my last breathe. As mentioned above, there is always a scope of learning and improvement which makes a person better. So always make a research on yourself and look for some courses, books or any way to improve you.

"Live as if you were to die tomorrow. Learn as if you were to live forever."
-Mahatma Gandhi

Even after following all these concepts, there will always be something left to learn and you can never predict 100% results or success. However, there are always some goals which you want to achieve. Many people do achieve their goals but they are not satisfied with it. As soon as they reach a milestone they look for something even bigger. It makes them feel unsatisfied or unhappy forever. Whatever efforts you make, there will never be an end point of your expectations. As discussed earlier, whenever we achieve anything, we starts craving for a bigger goal to achieve.

Everybody should celebrate their victory whenever they reach a milestone as there are many efforts, time and money is invested behind that. Celebrating the victory is another way of showing the respect towards your efforts.

Now that we have learnt about how should we work as an Individual let's take a glance into knowing about how should we work with others.

It's an unbreakable truth that we cannot escape of working with others. Whatever work you do wherever you go, you will have to deal with other people anyhow.

There is a huge reason behind it. There is no possibility that a person can do everything on its own; sometimes there are tasks which are difficult for one person to do and require the involvement of other person too.

Let suppose, if I want to start a business which requires some technical tasks to be done like creating a website and marketing. Now I am unable to do everything on my own as I am not a tech savvy person. So I will obviously need a person who can do this task for you. Many companies are using outsourcing for many of the important tasks as they are not able to manage everything on their own. This seems to be profitable as well. So anyhow, we will always need to deal with other people too.

This is again a learning thing for every one of us to make the things better and efficient.

Influencing or Compulsion

There are two major ways of working with others. When we work with others, there are situations can be there. One is we work for them, second is they work for us and last is working together for someone.

> **It is more important to influence people than to impress them.**
> **-Adrian Rogers**

Here if you want others to work for you in the way you want. There are two ways of getting this done. Either you can influence them about the work you want them to do or you can force them to do what you want. Either ways will get your work done. However, both the ways will have their own consequences.

If you try to influence someone that will give a positive effect to the person and the person will do what you want him/her to do by agreeing on your vision. The person will understand why you want him/her to do you want. And that person will have a good image about you. However, when you force anyone to do what you want, maybe the person will do it but that person will have a negative image of you and will never agree on your vision or point even if you are right.

Influencing makes the person understand the reason behind your ways to work and forcing creates the fear which let the person do what you want. In compulsion, the person will always try to find an opportunity to work somewhere else. As nobody likes to be threatened or being forced to do anything.

It's a human nature; nobody likes to be enforced to do anything. However, on the other hand influencing is the best way to let people work for you and the way you want them to do.

It is better that next time whenever you want someone to work for you in a way you want try explaining them about it.

Limited Team

Dealing or working with other people doesn't mean that you hire more and more people. When your team increases, communicating with everyone becomes more complicated. This affects the quality of work a lot. Because when people are more, there are chances of getting more disagreement on any decision needs to be made in favour of the organization or company. Everyone doesn't have the same point of view and that is why there is always an argument. To minimize this argument you need to minimize the people you need to communicate with.

When anything needs to be implemented, taking the approval from multiple people takes a lot of time and it highly affects the results. As sometimes there is a deadline of implementing the changes and in order to complete the tasks on time affects the quality of work.

This problem usually occurs in large companies, because large companies has a huge number of people where any small change has to be discussed between a good number of people and makes it slow to perform. The only solution to this issue is to minimize the number of decision making people. It will help in creating the transparency between the employees and higher authorities. Also, you will be able to complete all the tasks which get pending because of the lack of communication.

Showing Respect Equally

While you are working with others, it is really important to take care of everyone's pride. Giving importance to each and every employee in your company is the most crucial thing to take care off in order to build a good relationship with them.

Everyone likes to feel important and no one likes to be ignored or side lined. It is really crucial to show the respect and importance to the people's ideas and views. This makes them feel important and creates a good image of you.

If someone is using the phone, talking to someone else in-between and not listening to you properly will obviously make you feel ignored and less important. This destroys the relationship of people. And bad relationships can be the biggest cause of losses.

Respecting other people's time and pride is very important while working others. Let them feel safe while they are trying to put their views even though they don't match with your views. This makes them feel safe while speaking in front of you and they are able to express themselves openly.

> Equality is not in regarding different things similarly; equality is in regarding different things differently.
> -Tom Robbins

Cutting of in-between the conversation or arguments make them feel less important or unsafe. And this let me step out of conversation. This way they will never be able to express themselves and you won't be able to know what actually they want. Always give them space to talk about their views. Ask for their suggestions for any further improvements. Let them speak about their ideas and respect them.

Make other people feel good.

While working with others, it is really important how you are treating them. Making them feel important and safe is a basic part of it. Apart from this it is really needed that you show some appreciation and courtesy.

Even though if other person didn't do well which you wanted him/her to do. It is always a good idea to appreciate them. Always say "I can see, you have tried your best and did a lot of hard work on it however, you can still make it better. Let me get you some more good ideas". This way the other person will feel good about it and will do much better next time.

Showing courtesy is another good way of treating people. Being polite and pure with others make them feel good about you. They will always feel safe when they are around you and will be more cheerful towards their work.

Whenever you are assigning a task to someone or want other person to do what you want. Instead of enforcing anything it is always better to explain that why you want the person to do the task. Explain the logic behind it and why it is important to get this done. This way the other person will be able to understand that why you want them to do it.

This technique of making a request always works when you want other people to do what you want by explaining them that why it is important to get this task done. What is the logic behind this task?

Task Assignment and Planning

When any task needs to be assigned to a particular person in a group of people, you cannot go and ask the group to get a particular task done. As there are very less chances that anybody will be willing to do it voluntarily. So it is far better to assign the task specifically to a particular person to get the task done as soon as possible. People do not want to do anything extra voluntarily at all.

There are more chances that whenever you will assign a task to a group, every one of them will ignore it thinking that someone else will do it. However, when everyone has the mentality, the task left undone. So it is always important that if you want

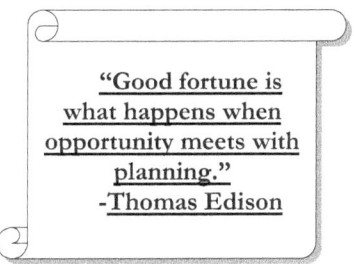

"Good fortune is what happens when opportunity meets with planning."
-Thomas Edison

to get a task done as soon as possible, assign it to a single person specifically rather than asking in a group.

Another common way of working is planning.

This sounds to be professional however, relying on planning is not always a good idea. Sounds awkward? I completely understand that since starting we have learnt that there should always be a plan before executing a task. This is ok that you make a plan but you cannot always rely on that.

To understand this, let's understand what is actually meant by planning. It is nothing but thinking of a future scenario and assuming the actions you are going to take which will complete the given task efficiently. And we all know that predictions and assumptions are not always true.

Which means no matter how accurate you are with your predictions, you cannot rely on them at all. Any emergency or any scenario can come anytime. You cannot see the future, your predictions might get wrong at any point of time and your plan may get failed badly.

So it is good to make a plan before executing any task but it is not at all good to rely on it as it cannot be 100% accurate ever.

Being in a Group

Since, childhood we have been taught to choose our surroundings, groups or friends wisely. Why it is like that?

This is because it's a human behaviour that whomsoever people spend their more time, it is very much possible that people adapt the same habits, thoughts and life style which most of their surrounding people have.

Whenever any kid starts going to school, to be comfortable in the environment the kid automatically looks for the friends who have the same kind of mentality, likes and dislikes and attitude. This is because everyone likes to be with people who are of same mind-set. And people who are of different mind-set, we try resisting to be with them.

Any person who is joining a new office, college or any new place starts making friends by making a judgment about them with the help of first impression. However, when they start knowing about the reality, there are obviously certain changes they make in friends group and sometimes change the whole group.

It is everywhere that people are divided into certain groups where every people in the group will have almost same mind-set and same lifestyle. It is very rare where you will find a person with average living standards having friends who live luxurious life.

It is very important to choose your group wisely because we all have certain visions and dreams in our life to fulfil. And to achieve our goals we cannot be distracted which is easily possible when we join a wrong group. Probably we like the people in a certain group as they have same likes as you. But sometimes when you are working to achieve your goal you need to ignore your likes and has to push yourself to achieve your goal. This will be very difficult for you to do if you keep yourself surrounded with wrong people who have same likes as yours.

Suppose, if you have a project to complete with certain deadline and you cannot afford to waste any of your time. Now you have a group of friends who all likes to party a lot as you do. However, in order to complete the project on time you cannot afford to be with them and partying. So you need to anyhow change your surroundings or be alone until you achieve your goal.

The same scenario works while you want to either have a new habit or need to quit an old habit. If anyone wants to quit smoking and your whole group loves smoking, trust me you will never be able to quit it completely until you are with them. Anyhow you need to reduce the time of being with them or maybe completely leave the group in order to quit smoking for whole life.

That is why everyone says, choose your friends, surroundings and group wisely.

Role Models

For any business, a role model is very important for the promotion of the services and product. You will see everywhere, every company do have a role model for promoting their brands, and they pay a huge amount of money to people to get the promotion done for their products. Why it is like that?

Have you ever tried to understand the reason or psychology behind it? Let me tell you, generally human tendency is like this, people do trust social proofs a lot when they want to buy something. It seems to them far safer to buy things when they see people using the same product or service and taking the benefits of it. When we see people taking some services and they are happy with it, it is more likely possible that we will go ahead and take the same service from the same provider as it feels more promising to us than taking a service from an unknown provider. That is why every company is keen to have more and more testimonials to close more sales.

When you see your favourite Actor, Sports Person or an Athlete is using a specific product, it gives you a trust that it is safe to consume any food product or use the same product which they are using even though in real life they don't use it. It happens with many soft drinks companies. Most of soft drink advertisements are being done by the celebrities and this helps the companies a lot in increasing the number of sales with a huge number. They advertise the product in such a way that consuming their product will also give you the same social status which the celebrity has.

It is very beneficial to have a role model for any product in order to build trust in your consumers to close more and more sales. This extensively helps the companies to bring more and more revenue. It is always worth of paying the role models, however every company needs to choose their models wisely, whom should be relevant for advertising their product. An athlete will never be a good choice for the advertisement of food oil. However, a chef will work better for the same.

Bound to take Action Indirectly

You must have seen, many companies who do provide online services including the applications, software, online streaming platforms do have subscriptions to pay. They don't ask you to pay altogether to get their services for lifetime. Instead they give you services on monthly payments. Here you are indirectly making a commitment to pay them every month. They offer you free services for some days and before availing those free services you would have to add your card details to make an automatic monthly payment. Now you are bound to pay them if you are using their services.

Similar way, when you approach a sweet shop, the salesman will always ask you to taste some of the sweets. Why is it so? Isn't that cost them? Yes it cost them but that is their strategy to put money out of your pocket. Whenever you are being offered something for free, your inner self will ask you to take something from them. You will feel bounded to complete your commitment of buying something from them. Many electronics showroom put their products on display for use. And whenever you approach the store, you will surely try using their products and you will indirectly make a commitment of purchasing something from them. That's how commitments with other people work in a business. When any salesperson makes efforts to show you what they are offering, you get the feeling that you should pay the person for their efforts by purchasing something from them. The similar scenario works in BPOs as well.

This is why many companies do offer incentives to their employees where every employee earns on the basis of number of sales they make in a specific period of time. When people do have incentive plan to earn, they are keener towards their work. They try their best to make more and more number of sales. Here the consistency of a salesperson becomes more rather than a salaried employee. An employee who is earning on commission basis will always work better than a salaried employee because the more sales he do the more incentive he will get. They get bounded to make more sales and ultimately, it benefits the company a lot.

Early Judgment

Suppose you assign a task to someone and give them a deadline to get the task completed. By any chance if the person doesn't complete the task on time, you will certainly get a negative picture of the person in your mind that in future you will never pick up the same person to get the task done.

In short you have got a very bad review about him/her. However, if we think about with the point of view of the person who got the task, we will get to know about the challenges he/she could have faced in order to get the task completed. Upon making a research we have got to know that the delay happened because of some unusual circumstances which were not in the control of the person.

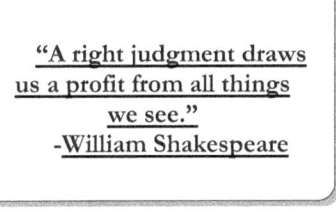

"A right judgment draws us a profit from all things we see."
-William Shakespeare

Now you will regret your decision about the mindset you got after looking only at one side of the coin. This is how sometimes early judgments backfires. So while making a judgment about other people, make a research and do proper homework before taking any decision. This will help you a lot in recognizing the people character and ability.

It is really very important that everyone should look at both sides of the coins before coming to a decision. Judging a book by its cover, always gives a wrong picture of the situation.

Availability

There is a saying, "Never be available always for everyone". Why it is like that? Because whenever you are always available whenever somebody asks anything from you, they stop respecting you and your time.

Suppose, if I receive a mail from my manager at late in the night and I replies on it at the same time clearly shows that I am available 24 hours for my work which will put my personal life on stake. Apart from that my time will never be valued; this will put wrong expectations to my manager that he/she can expect me to work anytime in the day.

This is not only in the case of professional life. The same scenario works in personal life as well. If your friend ask for any help from you at the time when you are at work, it won't be very good to respond him at the same time until it's a serious situation depending on one's priority. This not only disrespects you and your time but also creates a misconception for the other person that whenever next time they will need you, you will be available which cannot be the case every time.

Apart from this you also should be able to understand the situation too. You need to look at the priorities in every case. There is a possibility that you come across a scenario where you are unable to decide which task should be your first priority. In such cases, look at the situations carefully and see what can be the overcome if you miss any task, check which overcome or result you are able to bear if you miss any particular task to complete and go with the one which seems to be very crucial. One thing needs to be noted, there are still some scenarios which will make you think like crazy to decide, in those cases whichever task you pick up will work because there priority won't work. In those cases, you are like not able to move anywhere because both the situation seems important to you and you cannot ignore any one. In that case, go with anyone you feel like without thinking much about it. If you keep thinking a lot about it, the deadline will reach and you won't be able to work on either one. So it is better to work on either one.

Solution Oriented

I am working as a manager in a medical company, where I am reporting to the directors and I come across an issue where some of patients got a reaction through one of our products. This issue is being highlighted a lot in the market. Now, I need to work on it and reach our directors to inform about them about the issue.

There are two ways of it, where I can directly approach our directors with the issue and tell them what has happened.

What kind of response we can expect from our directors on this. Obviously they will be going to yell on me and get frustrated about it until they are very cool minded personalities.

> After every storm the sun will smile; for every problem there is a solution, and the soul's indefeasible duty is to be of good cheer.
> -William R. Alger

Another better way of approaching them will be quite different from the above one.

Here, I will be going to look at the possibilities of offering a resolution to our patients which I can present in front of our directors. So now I will think about 2-3 options which I can present in front of the management and let them decide the best one in order to get the issue resolved.

This way, the management will have a good and clear picture about the issue and the resolution. They will not be frustrated and hopefully the work will be appreciated too.
The learning is that everyone should be a solution oriented person. Problems are everywhere; if you look at the problems you will never be able to find a solution. And if you will look for solutions then you will surely find some. There is always a solution to a problem. No problem comes up without a solution and learning. It's all about how you look at the situations and present them to other people.

Management and Leadership

The most hyped job profile and skill nowadays is management and leadership which is the most important part of the company. Any company or organization cannot work without a good leadership and management. It always seems that these skills are very difficult to get and a person should at least be an MBA person who can have such skills. This is not at all true. These skills can never be taught in a class or in Academics. These skills come with experience. A good leader is not built in a class, they always comes from floors of an organization.

Let's understand what is meant by management. Management is nothing but a skill where one should be able to coordinate with a group of people in order to achieve a specific goal. Suppose there is a project which needs to be completed in an organization, firstly there is a set of people needs to be chosen who all can work together in order to complete the project before the deadline with the best quality.

Then we require a person who can coordinate with the group and help them out with the best ways to work on the project which is equally efficient and less time taking. Apart from this the person will also be making a plan before start working on the project. That person will be called as a leader or manager for the project.

Although the plan which has been built by the leader should not be concrete as we have learnt earlier. A plan can never be perfect because we cannot predict future. Constant changes have to be there according to the current progress. Every step of life or every challenge we face is a new learning for us. That is

"**A good objective of leadership is to help those who are doing poorly to do well and to help those who are doing well to do even better.**"

-Jim Rohn

why a plan can never be perfect however; it is an opportunity of learning for everyone. A leader should be an open minded person who allows every member to speak up about their ideas which might help the project. A closed minded person or a person who thinks he/she is the only best person to work on a project can never be a good leader or manager.

Being a Leader or a Manager:

- One should be recruiting the people with the best skills and qualities which will help the most in the project, keeping the shortest team to deliver best results as it should not affect the communication.
- Making a best plan which cannot be perfect and should be able to get amended when needed.

> "Good management is the art of making problems so interesting and their solutions so constructive that everyone wants to get to work and deal with them."
> -Paul Hawken

- Treating every one with whole respect and giving them complete chance to speak up about their ideas. Making them feel important so that they can be productive as much as they can.
- Creating an environment where everyone feels comfortable while working with least distractions.
- Helping the team members with the help of his/her experience whenever they stuck anywhere.
- Being available for them as much as he/she can.

A good leader is a person who keeps everyone on a same page and keeps the clear communication with everyone. Also, the person should be able to manage all the tasks to get the project completed on time.

Recruitment and Hiring

Here is the most important part of an organization. Where you need to search and look for the people who can work best for your organization. This process is not very simple;

hiring the best people can be as tricky as running an organization.

Like other organizations, to hire people firstly a job posting needs to be made where the job description should be self-explanatory, it should be representing all the roles and responsibilities which the candidate will have once hired. The job description should transparent enough to let the candidate decide where he/she will be the good fit for the position or not.

Once the job posting is done, there are loads of applications will appear where maximum people are not fruitful for the position and you need to filter out the best ones, this task is very tricky of making a judgment about the person. A bad hire can be a big loss for the organization as there is an investment which will be made on the candidate since hiring to training the person, providing the assets and resources, until the candidate is fully equipped to work for the company.

It is really important that we put a good filter while hiring the candidates from the applications received. Now to hire the best, look at the previous experience of the person. Check whatever they have worked into is it matching the profile you are looking for? Look for the candidate's previous achievements and projects. Make a thorough research on the previous profile. And when you are satisfied that the person's previous experience is matching the profile you are looking for then offer a short term project.

Once the offered task is completed by the candidate and you

are satisfied with the performance, you can go ahead with offering a full time job to the candidate.

Equality

While working in any organization at any post, you will deal with people of different levels and positions where obviously you will treat the people with respect and honor who are at higher levels by default. But what about the people who are at same level or below levels?

There we do not treat people in a very good way. Especially to those who are lower level, which creates a toxic environment for them and they start disliking you. They might do the work which you assign but they will never do it with the best of their abilities. If you are working as a manager and your attitude towards your team is not good. Trust me; your team will never be able to perform well. Being a manager, you have to show equal respect and honor to everyone to create a good image of yourself amongst them. Treating people is the most important thing which affects the performance of anyone.

> Democracy and socialism have nothing in common but one word, equality. But notice the difference: while democracy seeks equality in liberty, socialism seeks equality in restraint and servitude.
> -Alexis de Tocqueville

If you want your team to work with the best of their abilities and you want them to put 100% of their efforts, you need to show respect to them in terms of their work and time. You need to understand that they also have some personal life and the work which you are assigning to them should not affect it. Creating a good environment for them is your first job to do. Never let them regret their decision of working in your team or organization. And this not only goes with the agents you have. This works with each and every employee you have. Even a janitor deserves the same amount of respect. Never let them feel inferior. It is highly important to understand how we treat people while working with them. Be a personality who is empathetic and should be able to understand the situation of others too.

Notes:

3.

Understanding and Improving Structures of Business.

Now, as we have gone through that how we should work as an individual and with others. It is really important to understand the structure of a business and how can we improve it.

When we think about any organization, from outside it seems that a company has a very simple and sorted structure of working whereas in reality a company or an organization is a combination very complex structure where every structure is being run by people who have the expertise in the similar department.

A company which manufactures clothes is consists of many different departments starting from getting the right thread till the final product is ready to sell. It starts from getting the right thread or cloth, where the whole cloth need to be cut in right shape and size goes to stitching where stitching also requires multiple different processes to complete. After the stitching is complete, ironing and packaging also requires certain expertise when you are manufacturing a premium product. Once the product is ready to sell, marketing needs to be done in order to sell the product. So a simple shirt you are wearing has taken a lot of efforts in getting ready and sold to you.

It is very difficult to build the complete system from scratch altogether. A company or an organization has not been setup from scratch; it takes a lot of time and efforts for a company to be a company. Every organization has been started by creating a small structure. First a small structure needs to be created and worked on until it becomes perfect. Than step by step, other structures has to be setup and once there are multiple structures has been created and most of the things has been performed by the same company than it becomes a great organization.

Flow of Resources

When there is a system or structure, there is always an ongoing flow of resources, raw materials, money, end product will be there.

When you are in to manufacturing, there will always be some raw material, resources which will be in-flow in the organization in order to start building the product. People are hired which is an inflow of the company. Likewise, there are multiple things which are getting in and the same way there is an outflow of the products, money and employees for various reasons. Understanding this inflow and outflow is very important to run an organization.

This flow also refers to the stock. Stock is nothing but a pool of resources which are still there in the system. The stock has to manage very carefully. There should be a good understanding about the quantity of stock which is needed as per the situation. Because the quantity of stock is a very crucial part as both big and small quantity can be an issue depending upon the situation. The stock should be balanced as keep a big stock sometimes creates issues when the demand is not that thigh and maintaining the stock becomes costly. And when the stock is less and demand is high than you won't be able to fulfill all the demands.

Analyzing the lack in Stock

To manage the stock properly, it is highly important that we keep a check on the inventory and stock. Suppose you are in the production of laptops and you are getting short of the Mother Boards.

In order to complete the demands of the laptops, sufficient mother boards are needed to complete the demands.

You need to check if the stock of motherboards is enough or not. If it is not enough, you need to increase the production which you can do by asking the employees to work over time or on off days in order increase the production. There might be a situation where you would have to hire more people or buy more equipment. However, that might be very costly so need to check how much minimum you need in order to complete the task. Sometimes, you need more raw materials.

Once the production is increased, you also need to keep a check that production shouldn't go more than needed as it is taking more efforts and time. It should not be like that in order to increase the production of motherboards, the stock of screen is getting less. Re-evaluation is needed to check if every other thing is not lacking behind.

Keeping a thorough check on the inventory and stock is highly important in a system or structure.

Adaptable to changes in Environment

Whenever we talk about any structure, there is a rule where continuous changes will always be there. There is nothing fixed in this world. Somewhere changes in process and structure will always be there. However, people or businesses who are unable to adapt those changes cannot survive.

Let's understand this way, whenever you start feeling hot, it is pretty automatic that you will start getting sweat. Your body is designed to adapt the change in temperature. And sweat is there to prevent your skin from a burn. Same way businesses or structure of a business should be designed in such a way that it should be able to adapt the changes happening in the market.

In this huge uncertain market, no one can predict or see the future that what will be the change in prices of anything. Slight change in prices of fuel starts impacting all types of businesses and market. Almost all the businesses are using fuel in some way either in transportation or production. The structure of your business should be designed in such a way that such type of changes in the market should not be able to affect much to your number of sales or in any other way.

Every structure or business has a certain amount of criteria's where to run the business, those criteria's has to be met in order to keep the business.

A business needs a certain amount of cash flow in order to run a business. A certain amount of revenue, a certain quality matrices has to be met so that the business should not stop.

And the changes in environment should not affect those criteria's or if they are affecting it. The structure should be able to adapt those changes accordingly. No one can predict the future. Nobody knows what will be the price of fuel, stocks, shares or anything. The business or structure should be flexible to adapt all those changes.

Understanding the connections of Departments

Everything we use is mostly connected with different sources of energy. Anything which we use requires some kind of energy to run. Especially electronic products cannot work until they get electric energy without that they won't work at all. That is how the things we use depend on some outer source to work.

Same way most of the businesses are connected with different departments. To run any business, there are multiple departments involve. And each department depends on one other to achieve the final goal. If any department fails to deliver what it meant to deliver, it will affect other departments too and sometimes the whole business or structure as well.

Keeping as less departments or dependencies on one another as possible is the better way to run a business as this way the failure in one department should not affect other parts of the business.

Same way, when a business depends on too much outsourcing, it highly affects the business because if any of your contractors fails to deliver the value, it might delay the whole structure. Outsourcing is needed but too much outsourcing creates a high risk in a business. Keeping the dependencies and outsourcing limited makes any company or business stronger.

Analyzing Different structures and departments

As we know that there are multiple huge structures present in a business, it becomes very difficult for anyone to analyze such structures as these are the processes which cannot be stopped in between because of the dependencies. In order to measure the matrices and the quality of the process, these structures need to be divided into substructures and then examine them one by one.

Suppose if you are running a business of manufacturing bikes, it is hard to measure the complete performance of whole process in one go and even if someone tries to do it, they can never get the exact value and somewhere the measurement will surely lack. It is better that the process of manufacturing the bike should be divided in different departments. Which can be like a department of manufacturing the body of bike, one can be engine, one can be for breaks etc. And this way it will become easier to measure the performance of each department separately. This will also help in getting the precise value for all the quality matrices.

This is how it is always better to break down the structure into substructures in order to analyze the overall performance.

It is not always necessary to monitor each and everything. There are always some key indicators which need to be measured. This includes measurement of value creation, time being taken, and how many complaints in specific period of time. Anything which is affecting the performance of business in the visible manner should be monitored.

Moreover, you also need to understand that while manufacturing a product, the quality of the product will also depend on the quality of raw material you are using. If the quality of the raw material is poor, there is no way a possibility that you will get the best quality of final product no matter how much skilled labor, employees or machinery you are using. If you are manufacturing something where the quality of the final product matters a lot, the raw material should be of the same quality.

Choose wisely the key indicators in order to keep a track of the performance of your business.

Neglecting

Measuring a key indicator sometimes might have some errors. It is really very important to check and apply the buffer for neglect able errors. These are the errors which are not actually affecting the business and can be neglected.

As we know that there can never be anything which is 100% in this uncertain world. There will always be a scope of improvements. In such cases, when the performance for any structure, department or business is above 95% is considered to be as good. However, the percentage left are the errors which can be neglected and if you really want that the percentage of performance should be high which is quite possible but difficult. You can put more efforts, time and money in order to keep your performance up to 99.999%. Still 100% is impossible to achieve. So keep a buffer for those errors which can be neglected in order to achieve the goal which you have set up.

Auditing

It is highly important for a business or structure to do regular audits for different departments in order to keep a track of people, if they are working according to SOP or not. It is important to keep a check whether people are following the protocols of the organization or not.

Moreover, sometimes what happens is when an audit is being done and you come to know that there are some discrepancies which were being neglected earlier and you try to put that in front of the team. There is a possibility that it might show up as a negative impact on the team as nobody likes to be judged and sometimes you will be asked to keep it like that without making any changes on it. So that the team don't feel demotivated and keep those discrepancies as neglect able errors.

In such cases, a third party can be hired for audits where the emotions won't work and the needful changes will be executed without any further resistance. Because a third party won't have any emotional touch with the team and will be able to do audit honestly.

Comparison and Analyzing Output

Suppose if you have manufactured 1000 units of any specific product in this month. Generally, it seems to be a good amount however, if your production of last month was 2000 than it seems to be a bad deal. As when you compare it you get to know that the performance of your system is dipped by 1000 in one month. Comparing the performance with the past days, months or years performances gives a clear picture about the system's performance. Normally, the performance should always be improving from the previous months; still sometimes the performance do gets down due to some unusual circumstances. That is why auditing is important because it shows the clear picture that where the system is lacking behind and what is the scope of improvement.

Some businesses or systems are so huge that it becomes very difficult to analyze each and every product. In those cases, it is very helpful to check some of the random final products. This can be understood as you must have seen that whenever any phone company launches a new model, they do not check each and every single phone. So what they do is they distribute some of the sets to their team so that they can use it and give the feedbacks. Because that is enough to give the fare idea about the whole manufacturing system and is enough to analyze what needs to be improved. That is why many restaurants have random checks by the food critics, where they not only check the food but they also look after the customer support, servicing being offered to each and every guest. They also check how they are treating the people. These random audits give a fare idea that how the whole system is working.

Any packaged food company whenever needs to check the quality of their product they do not need to check each and every pack they are producing. They just give a try to some of them in order to check the overall quality and taste of the product which gives the fare idea about the whole production.

Changes for Improvement

In my company, the manager asked me to do an audit. After auditing I got to know that every employee who is handling the client is not keeping a record of the leads on the CRM system which is highly important. They are not doing that because earlier there were no as such strict instructions have been provided to keep a record. No such actions has been taken on it yet which means employees are habitual now of not doing it at all. In order to get this done, strict policy has to be made and regular auditing should be there because employees will take time to change their habits of working.

This is how making a change in the system can be difficult for anyone to adapt. In such cases, it is better to break a big change into smaller changes which can be applied slowly in the system where everyone will get enough time to adapt those changes. We cannot enforce any change to everyone so quickly as we need to understand that changes in habits takes time to get completely adapted.

Sometimes, whenever any new policy is being implemented and every one adapts it too. There is still a possibility that you might find some faults in that too after random audits.

You might find any employee not following the new policy, in such cases, there is no need to take any hard action on the employee and policy. A simple small discussion can work better on it. You can still try to make the person understand that why new policy is important and how it can help better to improve the overall structure of the company.

Changes in process to get more Output and Profit.

Sometimes, there are some changes needs to be made to increase the output of the business. The changes can be either in minimizing the input or maximizing the output in order to generate more revenue.

You can make the changes in the input where you can look for modern machinery which can work for you more efficiently and can produce more output in the same time. This also makes the business profitable even though the overall output is same. Or else you can increase the number of units being produced in order to overall increase the revenue by selling or serving more to your customers.

However, here everything doesn't need to be change; only one change can be very efficient.

In some cases, reanalyzing the whole structure again and after that making change in the process in order to be more efficient is also a good idea. This happens in the businesses, where technology is highly involved in the output. The technology can be improved on and on to make the process better for the same or better output. A machine which used to create 1000 units in a day earlier can be improved to create same number of units in 4 hours and then the same machine will create more than 2000 units in a day. This is how making changes in the system is helpful in increasing the output and revenue.

Analyzing the changes before execution

When we analyze the structure and we want to make some changes in the process in order to get more money. Any change should never be executed before calculating the result it might obtain.

Suppose, if any organization want to run more and more ads in order to get more clients but doesn't think about that if they have more pool of customers how they will cater all the demands. It is good to run more ads to get new customers but before that the business should be ready to deliver the best quality of business to the clients and customers. Once the demand is increased, the business should not lack behind in fulfilling those demands. So before making any changes to the system, all the parameters should be analyzed before execution which might affect the business in long term.

Business on Auto-Pilot

Everybody wants to have freedom in their life. Wealth with freedom can only be possible when you have a source of income which runs on Auto-Pilot. Suppose, if you are running a business which is making millions for you every month however, to keep it running you have to give 16 hours a day of your life to it. In these cases, wealth doesn't seem to be very good. If someone doesn't get time to spend money than what is the purpose of earning too much?

Everybody should get some time to spend the money they according to their desires and there is only one way out of it, having an income source which is on automation. Meanwhile, you can also work on making your business to run on automation. But how can you do that?

Whenever, any department or structure is built, it should be created in such a way where some of the SOPs have to be followed mandatorily by everyone and there should be a track of it. So it will let the employees know that what all they need to do on regular basis and there won't be any need to guide everyone every time. Removing the friction of uncertainty in the process let it work on itself until any external force is applied. Apart from that in the era of high technology, many companies are manufacturing the products through the automatic machinery with robotic access. Every machine is doing something in order to manufacture the product. There is a series of task which machinery has to do in such a way that after all the tasks are done, final product is ready to sell. The task starts from gathering the raw material to processing till packaging. Everything is being taken care off by machines with least human touch. This way, companies are able to manufacture more and more units in lesser period of time with least errors.

However, this process has to be monitored carefully as it can back fire the company very badly. Suppose if a company is in the field of manufacturing of chocolates. One part of the machine is responsible for adding milk to the solution with a specific quantity in a portion. Now if in case, due to some technical error in machinery if it starts adding more milk into the solution, there is a high possibility that it will create a huge damage to the production and cost. If the machine is able to manufacture 1000 chocolates in a minute, due to this error which is not identified within a minute can give a loss of 1000 chocolates. If one chocolate costs 10/- INR to the company. It will give the loss of 10,000/- INR in a minute. Any further delay is there in identifying the issue the loss will multiply minute on minute resulting in huge loss to the company.

Notes:

The End